BIBLE NUGGETS

JENNINGS (JAY) TURNER

WESTBOW
PRESS®
A DIVISION OF THOMAS NELSON
& ZONDERVAN

WestBow Press books may be ordered through booksellers or by contacting:

WestBow Press
A Division of Thomas Nelson & Zondervan
1663 Liberty Drive
Bloomington, IN 47403
www.westbowpress.com
844-714-3454

Because of the dynamic nature of the Internet, any web addresses or links contained in this book may have changed since publication and may no longer be valid. The views expressed in this work are solely those of the author and do not necessarily reflect the views of the publisher, and the publisher hereby disclaims any responsibility for them.

Unless otherwise indicated, All Scripture quotations are taken from the King James Version, public domain.

Scripture quotations marked (NIV) are taken from the Holy Bible, NEW INTERNATIONAL VERSION®, NIV® Copyright © 1973, 1978, 1984, 2011 by Biblica, Inc.® Used by permission. All rights reserved worldwide.

Scripture quotations marked (NKJV) are taken from the New King James Version. Copyright © 1982 by Thomas Nelson, Inc. Used by permission. All rights reserved.

Scriptures marked (NLT) are taken from the Holy Bible, New Living Translation, copyright © 1996, 2004, 2015 by Tyndale House Foundation. Used by permission of Tyndale House Publishers Inc., Carol Stream, Illinois 60188. All rights reserved.

Scripture quotations marked (MSG) are taken from THE MESSAGE, copyright © 1993, 2002, 2018 by Eugene H. Peterson. Used by permission of NavPress. All rights reserved. Represented by Tyndale House Publishers, Inc.

Any people depicted in stock imagery provided by Getty Images are models, and such images are being used for illustrative purposes only. Certain stock imagery © Getty Images.

ISBN: 979-8-3850-1734-8 (sc)
ISBN: 979-8-3850-1735-5 (e)

Library of Congress Control Number: 2024901206

Print information available on the last page.

WestBow Press rev. date: 01/17/2024

ACKNOWLEDGMENTS

Reading and studying the Bible has brought me many years of joy and peace. In the Word I have found unconditional love, mercy, grace, redemption, instruction and correction along with countless other blessings. I have recorded as "nuggets" incidents of blessing and insight that I believe have come from the Holy Spirit. My hope is that they will vie an encouragement and blessing to others.

I want to thank my wife Linda for offering her candid advice and support when proofreading the nuggets. Also, my sincere thanks to Linda Kaechele for her generous help with grammar, punctuation and content. Geri Stowman was also a help with grammar. The credit for anything contained in these nuggets that is good, true and of eternal value belongs solely to the Holy Spirit. Any errors contained herein are solely mine to bear.

Jennings (Jay) Turner

PREFACE

I have always viewed the Bible as a treasure chest. The contents of this treasure chest is far more valuable than gold or jewels. The Bible is the inspired Word of God. It is filled with love, truth, peace, salvation and is the primary way in which God speaks to us.

Scripture is not something that can only be comprehended by trained scholars. God is love. He loves each of us sinners and wishes to have an intimate relationship with each of us. There are various sources that can help us understand. In fact, many bibles have a running commentary that provides background, context and/or interpretation as you read. I highly recommend that you pray for guidance and a blessing each time you are about to read scripture. The greatest source of help for any of us to understand God's Word is his Holy Spirit.

I compiled these nuggets in the hope that they may be a blessing to the reader. They are intended to encourage, inform and inspire people to sit down with the Word of God and begin panning for eternal gold. The number of nuggets awaiting you is endless. What have you been panning for that is more important?

Anything worthwhile contained herein is solely due to God the Father, Jesus, his son, and the Holy Spirit. I am not some gifted scholar. I am a sinner saved by grace who loves the Word of God and wishes to share some blessings and encouragement. Please excuse my shortcomings in putting on paper what is in my heart.

Jennings (Jay) Turner

CONTENTS

GOOD SAMARITAN (PART 1 OF 3)
NUGGET 1

The parable of the Good Samaritan is found at Luke 10.30-36. Read the parable and then let's read it again from the viewpoint of law versus grace. We see that a man has been stripped of his clothes, wounded, and left half dead. The first person to come along is a priest. A priest represents organized religion. When the priest sees him, he leaves him dying and passes by on the other side of the road. Next, a Levite comes by and looks upon him. A Levite represents the law. The "Law" also passed by on the other side, leaving him to die. Next, we are told that a certain Samaritan comes along. The Samaritans were rejected by their brothers. This Samaritan is a type of Christ. Christ has compassion on us as the Samaritan had compassion on the dying man. This is an example of grace.

To me, this parable confirms that the "law" and "religion" will leave you dying. Now, let's look at what the Samaritan (Christ via grace) does. First he applies oil and wine to his wounds. Symbolically, oil and wine represent the Holy Spirit and blood. Next, he puts this man in his place by setting him on the beast. When you and I have received the Holy Spirit and have had the blood of Jesus applied to us, do we not also receive, by grace, the place belonging to Christ? Did He not, so to speak, step down to the earth for us? He then takes him to an inn and takes care of him. The next day before the Samaritan leaves, he pays the price of the mans care and promises to look after his future needs and promises to come again.

If our spiritual eyes are open, there are obvious similarities between the Samaritan and our Lord Jesus Christ. Without regard for himself, he helps a dying man, places the Holy Spirit and blood on him, elevates the wounded man to his place, pays the price of the man's wounds, promises to look after him in the future, and then promises to come again.

Make no mistake about it. Law and religion will leave you wounded and dying. Jesus wishes to pay the price for your wounds, no matter how grievous you believe them to be. The cure for anyone today who is spiritually wounded and dying is to, by faith, ask Jesus to apply the blood of His sacrifice upon your heart, thereby receiving the Holy Spirit.

Yes!

Jennings (Jay) Turner   2016

GOOD SAMARITAN (PART 2 OF 3)
NUGGET 2

—❦—

Let's look at the parable of the Good Samaritan again but from a different perspective. You can find the parable in Luke 10.30-36. This time, I would like each of us to imagine what each of the characters in the parable may have been thinking. I have listed below some thoughts. I have used this more than once in my Sunday school class and someone always comes up with another thought. I believe that the Holy Spirit may use this exercise to convict us of what our own motives may be when we choose to respond to a situation; or whether we respond at all. For example, what might the priest have been thinking when he crossed the street thereby avoiding being involved with the situation of the dying man? "I serve at the office".......

The Priest:

1. I serve at the temple.
2. If someone wishes to receive my services, they can come to the temple.
3. If this man has fallen prey to robbers, they may still be nearby. It may not be safe.
4. I will pray for him.
5. I will form a committee to study this problem.
6. Helping people in need is the responsibility of the government.

The Levite:

1. I have put in a full day at the office.
2. I cannot have contact with this man because he may be unclean.
3. I am not allowed to come in contact with blood.

The Thieves:

1. Finally, here comes an opportunity.
2. We need what he possesses for ourselves.
3. Let's strip him of his clothing. He won't have further need anyway.

The Samaritan:

1. I see a man in need of saving.
2. I will encounter sacrifice, but I love my neighbor.
3. I will bind him and make him a brother.
4. I will provide him a comforter who will help him until I return again.

The Host:

1. Another of the family has arrived.

There are doubtless other thoughts that you can think of that could be incorporated into the list above. Even general questions such as, "since the religious crowd obviously uses this road, why hasn't the crime rate been addressed?" Or, since the scripture tells us this man "was headed down", why hadn't the social programs worked on him (and the Thieves)? Maybe the guy had stopped by a local congregation but, since he was "headed down", he wasn't welcome and so he continued down the road he was on.

The main point of this nugget is that each of us would be wise to ask the Holy Spirit to open our eyes and hearts to understand our actions and motives from God's perspective with the hope that we will accept His will for ourselves.

Jennings (Jay) Turner   2016

GOOD SAMARITAN (PART 3 OF 3)
NUGGET 3

Some final thoughts concerning this parable: We are told that the Good Samaritan "had compassion" on him. Please consider that having compassion was not sufficient. His compassion led him to make "contact" with the troubled and dying man. Also recognize that this contact came with a "cost". His compassion led him to bind his wounds, apply his oil and wine, and then he transported the man. The opportunity to meet this man's need was right in front of him and he responded. Many people feel that recognizing an opportunity is the same as receiving a call. He didn't just remember him in prayer. That's not to say there is anything wrong with prayer. However, when an opportunity that we encounter is one in which we are capable of helping resolve, we should be sensitive to the guiding of the Holy Spirit.

Just remember this: true compassion will often necessitate contact and will have some form of cost associated with it.

What might be our individual reasons for not responding?

1. The person is not like me.
2. I serve at my church.
3. The individual appears to be undesirable.
4. This would be unpleasant.
5. I don't have adequate skills to be of assistance.
6. There are people who get paid to help with unpleasant things.
7. I don't want to get involved.
8. I wonder what sins have led to this persons predicament?
9. They may have made this bed they find themselves in.
10. ??????????

LESSON FROM JOB
NUGGET 4

In the first chapter of Job God asks Satan if he has considered gods' servant Job and how Job is perfect and upright. Satan states the reason Job is faithful is because God has blessed and protected him and that if Job were to lose everything he would curse God. In Job 1.12 God tells Satan that Satan has power over all that Job hath but that Satan may not put forth his hand upon Job. We then see that all of Jobs' oxen and asses were taken and the servants that were tending them have been slain. Next, fire has consumed all the sheep and the servants that had been tending them. Simultaneously, all his camels have been stolen and those tending them have been slain. Still in chapter one, his home has been destroyed and all of his sons and daughters have been killed. After all these things yet Job did not foolishly charge God. In chapter two, Satan tells God that although Job has not cursed God, if God will allow Satan to touch Jobs' bone and flesh, Job will curse God. God then allows Satan to "touch" Job but not to take his life. Still in chapter two, Job loses his health. In fact, he is stricken with boils from the soles of his feet to his crown. Although he wishes he had not been born, Job does not curse God.

A summary of some of the calamities the Job suffered include: his children died, the servants were slain, all of his livestock and crops were taken, his home destroyed, and he was in horrible physical condition.

Here, I think, is a nugget from Job: nothing happened to his wife. The reason? God sees man and wife as one. Therefore, if Satan could not take Job, then he could not take his wife.

When teaching Sunday school, I have put forth the thought that maybe his wife was left in an attempt to further his misery.

Jennings (Jay) Turner   2016

HEAD OF THE TABLE
NUGGET 5

Proverbs 25.6-7 tells us that it is better that it be said unto thee, come up hither; than that thou shouldest be put lower. Also, in Luke 14.7-11, Jesus says, "It is better to sit at the foot of the table and be asked to move to the head, than to sit at the head of the table and be asked to move." If your life can be seen as "your table," doesn't it stand to reason that Jesus wishes to be asked to sit at the head of your table? Although Jesus may be in your life, it appears clear that he wishes to be beckoned to a place preeminence in your heart, or, so to speak, at the head of your table. Conversely, if we later replace Jesus as the "head" of anything, including ourselves, are we not asking him to occupy a lower position? Wouldn't it be a great way to start each day by praying, "Jesus, I invite you to sit at the head of my table?"

Jennings Turner   2016

DO YOU ADVISE GOD?
NUGGET 6

Please read Numbers chapter 11. We read that God's people are dissatisfied with what He has provided for them. They continually seek after flesh and complain about the manna that God has provided. They dwell on some of the things they left behind such as leeks and onions. We can pray for God to guide us and to help us to seek what is best for us. This is preferable to just telling God what we desire and then relentlessly petitioning him for it. When God finally gave them flesh, there was a great penalty. It is wise for us to first be thankful for what we have. Next, we should always seek His wisdom and blessing concerning our plans and desires. There is nothing wrong with petitioning God. The key is maintaining an attitude in our hearts that wishes to know and accept His will. If you should ever find yourself in a position where you have strayed from God and are experiencing some chastisement, you might find the next nugget helpful.

Jennings Turner   2016

DIRECTION WHEN CHASTISED
NUGGET 7

Revelation 3:19 tells us, "As many as I love, I rebuke and chasten." What might we do if we have pursued a wrong path and find ourselves in a predicament as a result? What is our remedy from the effects of our straying? The obvious answer is to confess, repent and turn toward God. I want to paint a picture with words that, hopefully, will illustrate the wisdom in turning toward God, both from a practical as well as a spiritual perspective.

Imagine a young boy staying for a time one summer at his grandparent's farm. He is adventurous and occasionally mischievous. His grandmother is a very loving lady. Because she loves him deeply, she is willing to discipline him when he needs correction. He has needed correction a few times during his stay. The instrument of correction is a little willow switch. He finds his grandma to be an expert at its administration. Experience has taught him that if he runs, his backside is exposed and she has just the right amount of room and leverage to effectively apply the correction. He loves his grandma and knows that he deserved the chastening and that it has pained his grandmother not only that she has disciplined him, but that he strayed. He is a smart kid. He has learned that if he turns and runs to his grandma and hugs her to himself good things happen. While hugging her, she cannot effectively swing the switch toward him. Also, her heart is no longer in the correction. Thirdly, they feel their love for one another and his desire is to comply with her wishes because he knows they are in his best interest. This grandmother will be cherished and remembered with love his entire life.

In Matthew 23:37 we are told that God has often wished to gather His children like a hen gathers her chickens under her wings. Therefore, why not turn and run to Him and hug him?

Jennings Turner   2016

CORNELIUS AND THE GOSPEL
NUGGET 8

Please read the tenth chapter of Acts. Cornelius' alms, prayers, and his fear of God resulted in a holy angel coming to him in a vision. The holy angel tells him to send for Peter down in Joppa and that Peter will tell him what he ought to do to be saved. Peter comes and gives the gospel to Cornelius, his household, and all of his friends.

In that day, it would not have been a small endeavor for Cornelius to send three people to Joppa to fetch Peter. It would have been equally arduous for Peter and his party to travel to Cornelius, and presumably, back again. Question: rather than giving instructions requiring so much time and travel, why didn't the angel just reveal the gospel to Cornelius? I believe the answer can be found in I Thessalonians 2:4 that reads, "But as we were allowed of God to be put in trust with the gospel, even so we speak; not as pleasing men, but God, which trieth our hearts." The gospel is for us to share. Therefore, the angel could not. What an honor! What a responsibility!

The next nugget concerns a common fear that grips many Christians when they are presented with an opportunity to share the gospel.

Jennings Turner   2016

LESS FEAR WHEN WITNESSING
NUGGET 9

We have seen in the previous nugget that God has reserved the gospel to be spread by His elect (I Thessalonians 2.4). Our pastors are not "hired guns" whose primary responsibility is to go out and witness on our behalf. After all, their number is very small compared to the rest of us. Also, shepherds do not have sheep, sheep have sheep. This is not to say that pastors are not to witness, but clearly, each child of God should be ready and able to share the gospel. Christians of every stage of maturity seem to struggle with some level of anxiety and fear as they embrace the calling to share. Satan is the accuser of the saints. It seems that whenever we are willing to step out by faith to do God's will Satan is always there with doubts and thoughts of inadequacy. What if they ask me questions that I cannot answer? What if they or others ridicule me? The bible tells us that we are to be ready should any man ask us the reason for the hope that lies within us. Obviously, we should be able to show scripture that reveals God's provision for salvation. Additionally, every saved individual can simply give their testimony. Your personal testimony cannot be disputed as it is a recounting of your experience. Now, the gist of this nugget is to reason with you why our fear of witnessing is largely unfounded.

Many times in scripture the word of God is represented as seed. In the twenty-third chapter of Jeremiah, God's word is likened unto wheat while man's word is likened unto chaff. If you plant chaff it does not produce anything. Planting wheat may end up reproducing a hundred fold. The reason is that the seed is a creative thing. God's word also is a creative thing. You do not have to be a slick salesman in order "peddle the gospel." You do not have to be a great biblical scholar in order to effectively share your faith. God has this covered. He actually wants you to step out on faith. Romans 1.16 says, "For I am not ashamed of the gospel of Christ for it is the power of God unto salvation." Trusting God requires faith. Actually stepping out into what our fleshly fears tell us is a vulnerable situation is faith in action. This must be pleasing to God. James tells us that faith without works is dead. Works in the flesh is not profitable. You need God. If you wait to witness until you "know it all," you very well may never get around to it. Don't rely on your knowledge or ability. Using faith, depend on God. Knowing that the gospel is the power of God; shouldn't it embolden us to share?

Here is another nugget within this nugget. Seeds must be put into the ground and die before they "live" and produce a bounty. Jesus needed to die for us. He was put into the grave. He rose again. He has saved and continues to save God's bounty.

Jennings Turner   2016

AN ANGEL GIVES THE GOSPEL
NUGGET 10

Earlier, in "Cornelius and the Gospel," we saw why the angel couldn't give Cornelius the gospel. We read in I Thessalonians 2.4 that the saved were put in trust with the gospel. That was the reason the angel told Cornelius to send for Peter. Now let's look forward to Revelations 14.6. That verse reads, "And I saw another angel fly in the midst of heaven, having the everlasting gospel to preach unto them that dwell on the earth, and to every nation, and kindred, and tongue, and people." Is this a contradiction? Of course not! I believe that this is an indication that the saved are no longer on earth. This, I conclude, means that the "rapture" has taken place. If the saints were still on earth, they would still be charged with sharing the gospel. This appears to me to be strong evidence that the rapture will take place either pre-tribulation or mid-tribulation. In the next nugget I think we will see further evidence that the saints are in heaven prior to the second coming our Lord and savior Jesus.

Jennings Turner   2016

SATAN CAST FROM HEAVEN
NUGGET 11

Please read and consider Revelations 12.7-12. (7) "And there was war in heaven: Michael and his angels fought against the dragon; and the dragon fought and his angels, (8) And prevailed not; neither was their place found any more in heaven. (9) And the great dragon was cast out, that old serpent, called the Devil, and Satan, which deceiveth the whole world: he was cast out into the earth, and his angels were cast out with him. (10) And I heard a loud voice saying in heaven, Now is come salvation, and strength, and the kingdom of our God, and the power of his Christ: for the accuser of our brethren is cast down, which accused them before our God day and night. (11) And they overcame him by the blood of the Lamb, and by the word of their testimony; and they loved not their lives unto the death. (12) Therefore rejoice ye heavens, and ye that dwell in them. Woe to the inhibiters of the earth and of the sea! For the devil is come down unto you, having great wrath, because he knoweth that he hath but a short time."

We are told in the above verses that Satan is the accuser of the saints. This is revealed elsewhere in scripture as well. For example, read the account of how Satan accused Job before God. The book of Job tells us that Satan comes and goes before God with his accusations. In Revelation 12.0 we learn that Satan has been cast out of heaven. I think that the reason Satan has been cast out is because the saints are no longer on the earth. Therefore, the saints must be called up to heaven prior to the end of the tribulation.

Jennings (Jay) Turner   2016

FEAR OF THE LORD'S HOLINESS
NUGGET 12

When men encounter the holiness of God, they are overcome with fear. This is true whether they are saved or not. If unsaved, a glimpse of God's holiness cannot help but convict someone of their sinful nature. Christians also react with fear and trembling. Let's look at some examples in scripture. Read the first five verses of Isaiah chapter six. Isaiah is given a vision of the Lord sitting upon a throne, high and lifted up, and his train filling the temple. Isaiah's response to the vision is in verse 5, "Then said I, Woe is me! For I am a man of unclean lips, and I dwell in the midst of a people of unclean lips: for mine eyes have seen the King, the Lord of hosts." In the first chapter of Ezekiel, the heavens are opened unto Ezekiel and he is given visions of God and the glory of the Lord. In the final verse of chapter one, we see the result. Ezekiel says, "And when I saw it, I fell upon my face." Do you remember the story of the maniac of Gadara? It is found in the fifth chapter of Mark. We are told that this madman met Jesus and his disciples out of the tombs and that he had an unclean spirit. We are also told that fetters and chains could not hold him and that no man could tame him. Jesus, however, rebuked the unclean spirits which then entered into a herd of swine which ran violently down a steep place into the sea and died. When the people in the city and the surrounding area came out to see what was done and to see Jesus, they saw the man that had been possessed with the devil, and had the legion, sitting, and clothed, and in his right mind: and they were afraid. In Mark 4.35 Jesus, speaking to his disciples gets into a boat with them and tells them, "Let us pass over unto the other side." In verse 37 we find that a great storm arose and the waves beat into the ship so that it was full. Jesus, however, is in the hinder part of the ship asleep on a pillow. Verse 38 tells us that the disciples, afraid, wake Jesus and ask him, "Don't you care that we perish?" The question indicates that the disciples believe that their deaths are imminent. In verse 39 Jesus calms the sea. After seeing the sea has obeyed the word of Jesus, verse 41 says that the disciples "feared exceedingly". The disciples went from being afraid they would die to "fearing exceedingly." I think that this shows us that they were more afraid of the holy power of Jesus than their own death. Fast forward to Revelations 6:15-16. Here, the power and holiness of Jesus is being revealed to mankind. Those two verses read, "And the kings of the earth, and the great men, and the rich men, and the chief captains, and the mighty men, and every bondman, and every free man, hid themselves in the dens and in the rocks of the mountains; (16) And said to the mountains and rocks, Fall on us, and hide us from the face of him that sitteth on the throne, and from the wrath of the Lamb." Again, these people will desire death more than to be confronted with the holiness of God.

Remember that in Mark, prior to the storm, Jesus had told the disciples they were going to the other side. In spite of this, they focused on the storm around them. Is this due to a lack of faith? Do we not also focus on the storms of life? If you have read Revelation, you know how wonderful it will be for the saved of the earth. What is the difference between us and them? Don't we also focus on the storms of our lives even though we know our place in eternity? I believe the disciples were upset with Jesus and actually accuse him. They awoke him and asked, "Carest not that we perish?" Some Christians, during "storms" may question whether they are indeed saved. We may also question whether Jesus is with us during such times. He promises to "never leave us nor forsake us." It is not that our lives will be without waves, but Jesus will help us ride them. He also tells us we won't be burdened with more than we can bear. Don't let storms make you doubt your salvation. We know how it all ends. If you are going through a storm, it must not yet be the end. We must be careful to not focus so completely on our own doubts or situations that we fail to share the glorious gospel with others.

Jennings (Jay) Turner   2016

A PRACTICAL STRATEGY REGARDING CONFRONTATION
NUGGET 13

We know that Moses was very frightened when he was tasked with leading God's people out of Egypt. He put forth several reasons why he was inadequate for the job. Being inadequate was just what was needed because it would be God working through Moses that would accomplish the task. In Exodus 7.15 God commands Moses to "get thee unto Pharaoh in the morning." Exodus 8.20 says, "And the Lord said unto Moses, ruse up early in the morning and- stand before Pharaoh." Again, in Exodus 9.13, "Rise up early in the morning, and stand before Pharaoh." Three times God tells Moses to confront Pharaoh in the morning. Twice he is told to "rise early" to face him. I believe that we can learn from this that when we have a potentially difficult meeting with someone looming, it may be best for us to schedule it early in the morning. I spent many years as the CFO of a company made up of hundreds of employees. My position necessitated occasional confrontations that often involved a reprimand or even someone's termination. Such meetings were extremely stressful and I often fretted and procrastinated for days. During my daily bible reading, the Holy Spirit spoke to me through theses verses. My approach to these meetings changed. I would ask God to work through me to make such meetings as effective and comfortable as possible for myself and the other party. I also purposed that these meetings would take place as early as possible. While such meetings never became easy, trusting God's word dramatically reduced the stress. Any strategies gleaned from God's word that you are able to incorporate into your daily life are bound to give you more confidence, wisdom, and compassion.

Jennings (Jay) Turner   2016

SYMBOLIC LOOK AT SALVATION IN THE OLD TESTAMENT
NUGGET 14

According to God's instructions, the Israelites constructed a tabernacle, complete with a veil and an ark. God was very specific concerning materials and colors. Inside the tabernacle was an area designated as the "holy of holies." Someone entering into this "holy of holies" would be accessing God. The veil separating this space from the rest of the tabernacle weighed approximately 600 pounds, thereby preventing a man from entering on his own. Only once a year would the high priest enter this space. When the high priest entered into this inner room on the annual visit, it was to bring a blood sacrifice that he would pour onto the top of the Ark of the Covenant. The high priest had both bells and a rope attached to him. This was necessary because if he did something improper he would die. The rope was to allow his body to be removed. Only the high priest could enter so helpers would not be able to go in after him. The occasional sound of the bells would let those outside know that he was still alive. The Ark contained three items: a portion of the wilderness food (manna), Aaron's rod that budded, and the broken tablets of the law. The color of the veil was blue, purple, and scarlet. The veil is a type of Christ. Blue for deity, purple for royalty, and scarlet for sacrifice. If all went well, the sins of this people would be forgiven for a year. This is really a picture of the blood sacrifice of Jesus yet to come. You see, when God looked down upon his broken law (the broken tablets were in the Ark), he saw it through a blood sacrifice. If you look at Matthew 27.51 and Mark 15.38 you will see that immediately after Jesus has given his life, the veil is "rent in twain from top to bottom." This is because now the believer has direct access (without the priest) to God by "passing through" Jesus (the veil).

Next, I would like you to consider some similar aspects that occurred during the Passover. Again, we see a picture of Christ in the spotless lamb that is to be slaughtered. Jewish custom even required that the lamb be skewered once through the shoulders and once lengthwise.

Would that not form a cross? The blood of the lamb was then to be applied to the door posts using a branch of hyssop. Hyssop is a symbol of faith. Therefore, by faith, the blood sacrifice of the lamb was to be applied to the door posts. Consequently, when the death angel looked upon such a house, he saw it through the blood and "passed over" the home.

Here is the good news (gospel): by faith, you can apply the blood of Jesus, so to speak, to the door posts of your heart so that God will see the blood of Jesus instead of his broken law (sin) when he looks upon you.

Jennings (Jay) Turner   2016

YE HAVE NOT YET RESISTED UNTO BLOOD, STRIVING AGAINST SIN
NUGGET 15

The title of this nugget is from Hebrews chapter 12, verse 4. In verse 3 we are told that if we feel wearied or faint we should consider Jesus. After all, we are told, Jesus suffered the greatest contradiction: that is, he suffered sinners against himself. Jesus, with no sin, took upon himself our sins, then suffered sinners to judge him and execute him so that his sacrifice would be the price of our redemption.

I don't think that the greatest suffering that Jesus endured for mankind was the ridicule, physical beatings, or the execution he experienced. Jesus was fully man and fully God. Lightness and darkness cannot occupy the same space. Nothing can be more opposed than holiness and sin. For a holy Jesus to take on sin must have been the most difficult thing that could have ever been contemplated. In addition, God the Father had to turn away from the Son so that he would not look upon the sin that was placed upon Jesus when he received the sins of the world upon himself. Can you imagine the difficulty of a completely sinless, righteous and holy Jesus accepting sin? To paraphrase verses 3 and 4 of Hebrews chapter 12; if you or I find ourselves weary of the battle, we should consider Jesus, who did resist sin unto blood. We, who have all sinned, have never resisted to this extent. I believe that this reference is to Luke chapter 22, verse 44 where we find Jesus in the garden on the night of his betrayal. Here, Jesus is in agony, not at the prospect of the physical trauma to come, but at the eventuality of his holiness taking on sin as well the result of that meaning that God the Father would temporarily forsake him. Verse 44 suggests that Jesus sweat great drops of blood. Hebrews 12.4 says "Ye have not yet resisted unto blood, striving against sin." I believe Luke shows us that Jesus, in fact, did.

Chapter 12 of Hebrews instructs us, when we feel faint or weak in our walk, to consider the great cloud of witnesses (all of Hebrews chapter 11) who have gone before us and to also consider Jesus who suffered sinners against himself. Doing so will surely help us to withstand any storms that surround us. What a savior! Think of it.

Jennings (Jay) Turner   2016

SACRIFICE FOR ISAAC
NUGGET 16

In Genesis 22 God did test Abraham when he asked him to make of Isaac a burnt-offering. In verse 7 Isaac asks his father "where is the lamb for a burnt-offering." In verse 8 Abraham answers "God will provide *himself* a lamb for a burnt-offering." When Abraham was about to slay Isaac, the angel of the Lord called out and told him to not harm the lad. In verse 13 Abraham looks up and sees a ram caught in a thicket of thorns by his horns and Abraham offered it up as a sacrifice. Indeed, God did *provide himself* when he gave Jesus as a sacrifice. Was not the ram symbolic of Jesus? A ram (male lamb) becomes the sacrifice. Also, this sacrifice had thorns on his head as did Jesus.

A blood atonement is repeated over and over in the bible. In Genesis Chapter 3, Adam and Eve have eaten of the tree of the knowledge of good and evil. Their eyes have been opened and they know that they are naked. To hide their nakedness, they have sewn fig leaves together and made aprons. They have also hidden themselves from God. God, of course knows where they are. Still in Chapter three, God made coats of skins, and clothed them. Something obviously died in order to make clothing from skins. Later, Abel sacrificed of his flock and it was acceptable. Cain brought of the fruit of the ground for his offering and it was not acceptable. God exhorted Cain to bring a sin-offering but he would not.

A last thought here. Adam, obviously a brilliant man, tried, to no avail, to hide from God. Are you now or have you ever tried to hide from God? If so, how is that going for you?

Jennings (Jay) Turner   2017

PEOPLE ARE FOR LOVE
NUGGET 17

As Christians, we are in the business of love and forgiveness. In Galatians 5.22 it lists the fruit of the Spirit not fruits. Love is the first item listed. Since "fruit" is singular, I assume that all the rest are offshoots of love. Matthew 19.19 tells us that we are to love our neighbor as ourselves. Matthew 5.44 even tells us to love our enemies. It is clear what our duty is toward people.

Isaiah 44.9 says,"They that make a graven image are all of them vanity; and their delectable things shall not profit." Things are just things. Clearly, we are not to worship things. The Israelites are asked why they would worship something that cannot speak nor hear.

I want you to consider the following:

GOD GAVE US PEOPLE TO LOVE
AND THINGS TO USE, BUT
IF WE LOVE THINGS,
WE WILL USE PEOPLE

Jennings (Jay) Turner   2017

FOLLOWING CHRIST
NUGGET 18

The Lord Jesus Christ, both God and man, gave up everything so that he could serve people and ultimately sacrifice his life for the ransom of many. Jesus was not self-centered. He virtually lived an other-centered life. In Matthew 20:27 we are told,"whoever will be chief among you, let him be your servant." We are instructed in Galatians 5:13 that we should "by love serve one another."

Jesus, in Mark 8:34 says, "Whosoever will come after me, let him deny himself, and take up his cross, and follow me." If we are to follow Jesus, we must become other-centered. It will require more than a committee and a prayer. I believe it will require compassion, love, and contact. Usually, seeing an opportunity to be of service is receiving a call to serve.

Jennings (Jay) Turner   2020

SALVATION TRAIN
NUGGET 19

As I grew in my walk, study and service, God has helped me to grow closer to him and to trust him more fully. I still have a strong desire to be in control. I have tried many times to hand over control to him and not intervene with my own input. This has been a battle and remains one. I am an old bean counter (CPA) and my mind tends to work in logical progressions. My first premise is: is God real? This is an easy beginning for me since I have always been certain of it. I can see Him all around me in nature. His Son testified of Him. His Holy Spirit lives within me. I have noticed that even the trees lift up their arms to him. My second question is: does He love me? Well, He gave His only Son to die for me as a sacrifice for my sins. Thirdly, does He know my needs and wants? Scripture tells me that He knows me better than I know myself. He is my creator. Therefore, who could know me better? I have made many decisions in my life without consulting God. I can tell you that most of them did not turn out as I had envisioned. Even when I have sought his will, I believe most of the time I wanted to know what his plan was so I could then decide if it fit in with my idea. I now realize why I couldn't "hear" his will. I don't think he was interested in me testing him. Hopefully, we come to a place where we realize that he loves us more than we can ever comprehend. He has and does pursue us. He knows what we need better than we do. He wants the most fulfilling life possible for us. It is at this point where our attitude may finally be one of "all in." We need to quit trying to direct everything on our own. Put no so called "gods" before him. At this point in my life, I see this as an analogy of "getting on board the train." I have read Revelation so I know the tracks that this train rides on ends up in heaven.

Now, back to the train analogy: I visualize the tracks may go through tunnels and valleys, over mountains and across rickety bridges but I believe that the journey is going to prepare me for the destination. I want everyone to get on board this train. There is plenty of room for anyone with a ticket. The tickets are even a free gift. Jesus is happy to issue anyone a ticket regardless of anything in your past. Give up trying to pick your own roads and deciding which fork to take. The engineer that laid these tracks is perfect. The conductor loves us more than we love ourselves. He shows all the passengers the majesty and holiness of the creator as we are on this journey and urges each of us to invite as many people as possible to come aboard the train.

ALL ABOARD! Don't be left at the station.

Jennings (Jay) Turner   2017

LAZARUS CAME FORTH
NUGGET 20

In John chapter 11 verse 38 we find Jesus at the grave of Lazarus. It was a cave, and a stone lay upon it. In verse 39 Jesus says, "Take ye away the stone." In verse 43 Jesus cried with a loud voice "Lazarus, come forth." Verse 44:"And he that was dead came forth bound hand and foot with grave clothes; and his face was bound about with a napkin. Jesus saith unto them, "Loose him, and let him go."

Obviously, Jesus, being able to raise Lazarus from the dead, could have also rolled away the stone and loosed him from his bonds. Instead, he had his followers roll away the stone and loose him. Could it simply be that Jesus had his followers do those chores because they could? Does God expect us to do what we can do?

Jennings (Jay) Turner   2017

SHADOW IN THE VALLEY
NUGGET 21

Psalm 23:4, Psalm 44:19 and Job 3:5 all refer to either the "valley of the shadow of death"; or "shadow of death." Consider this: how could this shadow be around us unless there be a great light to cast it? Please take heart and remain confident in God's love and concern should you find yourself in a valley or in a time of darkness. Keep looking unto Jesus, the author and finisher of our faith.

Amen.

Jennings (Jay) Turner   2017

SMYRNA
NUGGET 22

Revelation 2.8-11 is the message to the church of Smyrna. Of the seven churches addressed in chapter two, God recognizes their good points but yet finds something against each church except Smyrna. This church went through tribulations and persecution and was crushed. These circumstances no doubt purified the congregation. Church goers who were members in name only would have left when persecuted thereby leaving a sanctified membership.

In Matthew 2:12 we see that one of the gifts brought by the Magi to the young Jesus was myrrh. Myrrh is the root of "Smyrna". Myrrh contains a sweet savor but in order for the savor to be released, it must be crushed. The connection here is that Jesus would have to suffer (be crushed) for us. Our savior had to die in order for mankind to have a remedy for sin. Romans 6:23 says, "The wages of sin is death." Wages are what you earn. The last half of Romans 6.23 tells us that the gift of God is eternal life through Jesus. The sinless life of Jesus made it possible for him to be a substitute for us. He was able to pay the price in full for our sins. He suffered for us and in doing so, he released the greatest savor imaginable. No matter how great your sins, he died to pay the price in full for anyone willing to accept him as Lord.

Don't wait even a minute for anything. Make that decision now. Don't for a minute think you need to "clean up" yourself before opening the door of your heart and inviting him in. Jesus came to save sinners. Many of the disciples who came to Jesus were considered by most of society as undesirable. We are *all* sinners. Without Jesus everyone is lost.

The church at Smyrna suffered in the human sense but prospered in the spiritual and eternal sense. Therefore, stand firm and hold fast to our Savior.

Jennings (Jay) Turner   2017

REACH UP
NUGGET 23

When a hurricane or other storm has passed by, the plants in your garden are pretty well smashed down. In recovery, they begin to reach up to the sun.

Damaged plants reach up to the sun.

Damaged people reach up to the Son.

Jennings (Jay) Turner   2017

THE BODY OF CHRIST
NUGGET 24

Every believer is a member of Christ's body. 1 Corinthians 12-13 says, "For as the body is one, and hath many members, and all the members of that one body, being many, are one body, so also is Christ. For by one Spirit are we all baptized into one body, whether we be Jews or Gentiles, whether we be bond or free; and have all been made to drink into one Spirit."

I see this as meaning for now, we each have various gifts and abilities and we are to work together in concert. This means we should be of one mind and Spirit and "fitly framed together." We will eventually each be a cell in the Body. That is, the body of Christ.

In Matthew 22.23-33 the Sadducees came to Jesus and said that under the law, if a man should die without leaving seed, his brother should marry his wife and raise up seed to his brother. This goes on for seven brothers so that in the end, the woman has been married to all seven brothers. She then dies. The question of the Sadducees to Jesus is, "in the resurrection whose wife shall she be of the seven?" Jesus tells them, "In the resurrection they neither marry, nor are given in marriage, but are as the angels of God in heaven." It goes on to say, "God is not the God of the dead, but of the living." We have a physical body that is often referred to as the "outward man." There is also a spiritual man inside us. When Jesus says that we must be born again, it is this spiritual man that is reborn. We become a "new creature" or "new creation." The New Birth is a new creation from above changing your spirit completely when you truly repent and turn to God. This new creation is brought about in the following manner: 1. You must understand that you are a sinner (see Romans 3.23). 2. Admit that Jesus Christ shed His own precious blood to save you from your sin (John 3.16); 3. Understand that only grace, not works, can save you (Ephesians 2.8-9); and 4. Believe and confess (Romans 10.9-10).

When someone is born again, John 1.12-13 tells us, "But as many as received him, to them gave he power to become the sons of God, even to them that believe on his name: Which were born, not of blood, nor of the will of the flesh, nor of the will of man, but of God." It is your inner spirit that is born again. The inner spirit of a human never dies. Many people believe in God but he is Father only to his children. If your spirit has been reborn, you are a child of God and you will in no wise be cast out (John 6.37). One day in heaven, you will be part of the amazing family and body that will exist in perfect harmony full of love.

If the Holy Spirit is tugging at your heart, please do not delay.

Jennings (Jay) Turner   2017

HOW BIG IS YOUR GOD?
NUGGET 25

Have you ever considered the size of God? He is a spirit but think about everything He has made plus the entire universe and all that is in it! His creation, holiness, and accomplishments are so amazing that it is overwhelming to try and take it all in. This begs the question; if your God is so big and remarkable and He lives inside you, shouldn't He stick out? Shouldn't others be able to see the evidence of God residing in you?

If you have experienced salvation, you are a new creation and the Holy Spirit resides in you. There is a peace and rest that comes from your salvation. A great weight was lifted from you. As this "new creature" matures, there is another peace available to you. It is the peace that comes from submitting your will to Him. It is very hard for most of us to yield control to anything or anyone. God loves us beyond what we can imagine. If by faith we trust Him and desire Him to guide us, He will lead us into the most fulfilling life possible. Luke 11.11-13 says, "If a son shall ask bread of any of you that is a father, will he give him a stone? Or if he ask a fish, will he for a fish give him a serpent? Or if he shall ask an egg, will he offer him a scorpion? If ye then, being evil, know how to give good gifts unto your children, how much more shall your heavenly Father give the Holy Spirit to them that ask him?"

You can trust God never to lead you in a wrong direction. There is peace to be found when you trust enough to "let go." When you decide to go "all in," there is a peace that comes from finally yielding to the "prods" of the Holy Spirit.

Jennings (Jay) Turner   2017

SEARCH FOR GOD'S METHOD
NUGGET 26

In "The Message," a translation by Eugene Peterson, Isaiah 2.3 reads: "They'll say, Come, let's climb God's Mountain, and go to the House of the God of Jacob. *He'll show us the way he works so we can live the way we're made.*"

How often have each of us made choices that didn't work out the way we had hoped? We continually make decisions based on things like feelings, or what the world projects as success. Television shows and commercials continually present us (usually subtly) with the impression that we will find fulfillment in a certain car, a cool style, fancy home, more money, etc., etc. We keep thinking something "down the road" will give us peace about why we're living. "When I get that promotion," "when I retire," "when the house is paid off," "when the kids are gone and settled in," and on and on.

Whom do you think knows best: you, the marketing people of the world, or perhaps *THE GOD OF ALL CREATION WHO MADE EACH OF US?* To paraphrase the verse above, if we will go the House of God and seek knowledge, he will show us his ways so that we can live the way we were made. Seek to know His ways and then if we yield to his ways we can be on course for the most fulfilling life possible.

Proverbs 14.12: "There is way which seemeth right unto a man, but the end thereof are the ways of death."

Jennings (Jay) Turner   2017

DO YOU HAVE THE RIGHT LEG TO STAND ON?
NUGGET 27

Isaiah 7:9 (KJV) reads; "If ye will not believe, surely ye shall not be established." This same verse in Eugene Peterson's translation into contemporary language reads, "If you don't take your stand in faith, you won't have a leg to stand on." We all have a basic need to feel secure and this basic need drives us to seek security. Unfortunately, most of us have tried, and are still trying, to find security in things that seem to the natural mind to be able to provide this need. We seek many things in the natural man that our flesh and the world tell us will both satisfy us and make us secure. We aim at money, position, fame, etc., etc. We could all name a few. There is nothing wrong with having, for instance, money, a nice home, or a great job. If God has so blessed you, praise Him! You just can't love them more than Him. If any of these things have become what you "stand" on, then they have become your god. It requires faith in order to stand on God. You simply cannot please God without faith.

Jennings (Jay) Turner   2017

ARE YOU AN IMPLEMENT?
NUGGET 28

In the KJV, Isaiah 10.15 reads: "Shall the axe boast itself against him that heweth therewith? Or shall the saw magnify itself against him that shaketh it? as if the rod should shake itself against them that lift it up, or as if the staff should lift up itself, as if it were no wood."

This same verse in The Message reads: "Does an ax take over from the one who swings it? Does a saw act more important than the sawer? As if a shovel did its shoveling by using a ditch digger! As if a hammer used the carpenter to pound nails!" The scripture is referring to the King of Assyria whom God used for punishment but was "puffed up," full of pride and claiming everything that had happened was accomplished solely by his own power. I think it is a good idea to look at this from the standpoint of what can be accomplished by we believers.

Each believer should view themselves as a possible tool to be used in the hands of our Lord. If we allow ourselves to be used by God, and anything eternal is accomplished, we must give Him all the glory. A hammer or nail doesn't take credit for a building.

Now about being used: each and every believer has the ability to be used as a tool by God. What good is a hammer if it never leaves the tool box and is never used for the purpose for which it was created? When Abraham was called, he answered "Here am I." Are you "all in?" It requires faith to allow yourself to be a "tool." God has your back. Just step out in faith. You cannot accomplish anything nor can you please Him without faith. He loves you more than you love yourself. Would a loving father ever not give you all the support needed? Please don't view this as a guilt trip. Being used for the purpose for which we were created leads to a fellowship filled with joy.

Jennings (Jay) Turner   2017

CAN ANYTHING COMPARE TO GOD?
NUGGET 29

Isaiah 46.5 says, "To whom will ye liken me, and make the equal, and compare me, that we may be like?"

Our God is so holy and great that we cannot envision Him. I'm sure that we have all tried in our minds to picture Him but in so doing, we lessen and reduce Him because God is beyond our imagination. When, in Isaiah chapter six, Isaiah is given a glimpse of God's holiness, he falls as though one dead and is completely undone. The Holy Spirit directs us to Jesus and Jesus to God the Father. Take a deep look into Jesus to get an idea of God.

Whatever problems you are facing, remember that Jesus died on the cross so that His blood could be the atonement for your sins. God gave us this unfathomable gift by grace so that we may receive salvation freely without works. That is a love so profound that I can only marvel at it and praise Him for His great mercy.

Jennings (Jay) Turner   2017

IS GOD YOUR STRENGTH?
NUGGET 30

Chapter 49 of Isaiah tells of Christ, the future redeemer of both Israel and the gentiles. God says that Christ is honored in God's eyes and will be used mightily. In chapter 48.14–16 God has called Cyrus to be His tool. God says that He is using Cyrus and that Cyrus will be successful. What an amazing privilege to be used of God and be honored in His sight. God gave assurance that Cyrus would be successful. Obviously, the same is true for Christ. If we make ourselves available for His use, won't we also be successful? Works are essential to our growth and to the accomplishments of the true church; i.e., the Body of Christ. Each of us should be available to be used for any use we believe God would wish us to be involved. If we are used by Him, we can rejoice that we were an implement used in accomplishing His goals. Works without Him are temporal.

Jennings (Jay) Turner   2017

WHERE DO WE PLACE OUR HOPE?
NUGGET 31

In the last sentence of Isaiah 49.23 (KJV), God says, "for they shall not be ashamed that wait for me." In The Message, the same sentence reads: "No one who hopes in me ever regrets it." I have never known anyone who, after studying the scriptures, didn't conclude that they are inspired by God and just as current for today as when first penned. The Word gives me great hope and joy even when I am corrected by it. I find peace and direction for my future. I can scarcely take in that the creator of the universe loved me so much that He gave His son as a sacrifice to make possible my salvation. My hope is in my future resurrection. I have confidence and faith in the scriptures. According to the word of God, I will not regret it.

What is your hope based upon? I am very flawed. I fail every day. As hard as I try in the flesh, I am weak. The good news (gospel) is that Jesus died to pay the price of my sins. When I accepted Jesus as my Lord and savior my sins were forgiven. His blood covers my past, present, and future sins.

Some people feel that they need to "clean up" before seeking Him. It is only by His grace we are saved. His grace is sufficient for whatever you have done or been through. An old hymn says, "just as I am without one plea, except thou blood was shed for me." Another says, "in my hand no price I bring, simply to thy cross I cling." We are talking about the difference between eternity with or without God as well as a source of peace while we go through the many trials of this life. If, at any time, you feel a prompting by the Holy Spirit, please do not delay. We are told that if we seek Him, we shall find Him.

Jennings (Jay) Turner   2017

ARE WE PATIENT ENOUGH?
NUGGET 32

In Luke 19.35-38 we see the story of Jesus' entry into Jerusalem. We see in these verses that His disciples and the multitude spread their clothes and palm fronds in the way for Him to ride upon. In verse 38 they cried out "Blessed be the King that cometh in the name of the Lord: peace in heaven, and glory in the highest."

There was a problem. The people's idea was that this King would fix their worldly problems such as freeing them from the oppression of Rome. They imagined He would bring justice and make everything "right." They didn't realize that Jesus came to be a sacrifice for their sins, thereby providing an opportunity for eternal life.

I think there is somewhat of a parallel for us when we have prayed about or for something and the answer is slow in coming or perhaps is answered in an unexpected manner. When we don't receive an answer in our expected time frame, have you ever thought: 1) He didn't hear me, 2) I am unworthy to approach Him, or 3} I am incapable of hearing Him? If the answer doesn't come by the time we think it should, do we ever turn to our own resources in order to resolve the issue? E.g, throw money at it or launch ourselves into our preferred solution? In fact, if we think we have heard an answer but it doesn't coincide with what we expected or desired, do we ever try to achieve the outcome we desire? If we go with our own resources, aren't we pretty much turning away from His solution much the same way the disciples did when the "King" didn't come to fulfill their expectations in the way they desired?

As far as point "2" above, don't ever think you are unworthy of God's salvation. Receive Jesus as your lord and savior. Nothing you have ever done or thought of can be too great for His Grace and blood to cover.

He died for YOU. Don't for a moment attempt to "clean yourself up before approaching Him." He wants your spiritual man to be reborn. Only He can do it. He loves you and wants you right now, just the way you are.

Jennings (Jay) Turner.   2017

WE KNOW HOW IT ENDS
NUGGET 33

I assume that a portion of the rebuke Jesus gave the disciples on the boat concerning their lack of faith stemmed from the fact that Jesus had told them when they boarded the boat that they were going to the other side. After the calming, they immediately reached the other side. Read the last chapter of Revelation. We know the ultimate destination of those who have put their trust in Jesus. God has revealed how it ends. Faith in this knowledge should help us through the storms of this life. If it's not okay now, then it must not be the end.

Jennings (Jay) Turner   2018

VISIT OF THE MAGI
NUGGET 34

Matthew 2.11-12 tells the story of the Magi coming to bring gifts and worship Jesus. The scripture says that after they found Him, they went a different way. God first loved us and has mightily pursued each of us. The only way to God the Father is through His only begotten son, Jesus. If you have found Jesus, just as the Magi, you should go a different way.

One of the worship songs says, *"I'm running to your arms."* God tells us "if you seek me, you shall find me". That is the direction each of us must go in order to live our lives as God intends. It is the path where we find true fulfillment, joy, and eternal life with Him. This path will not be without troubles and trials. Some friends and even family may not understand and may even shun you. Many, many people believe that *happiness* comes from *happenings*. Joy can be in you regardless of circumstances as long as you can see life from an eternal perspective.

If you are on any other path, all you have to do is turn His way and He will direct you and you can experience this joy that is not dependent on circumstances.

Jennings (Jay) Turner   2018

CRISIS PRAYERS
NUGGET 35

In Jeremiah 11.14-16 (The Message), God says He is not going to listen to crisis prayers. He also says, "Do you think making promises and devising pious programs will save you from doom? Do you think you can get out of this by becoming more religious?"

The context here was God speaking, through Jeremiah, to His people, Israel. They have been helped by God over and over and as things become calm, they turn their backs on Him and worship other gods.

A lesson from this for each of us would be not to wait until you are distraught and without any peace about what is happening before you reach out to God. Our natural man wishes to be in control of every aspect of our lives. We desire, so to speak, to be the captain of our ship. However, if the ship has hit an iceberg or is about to go aground, in our crisis, we cry out to God. What if we had asked God to be our captain or maybe the Holy Spirt to be our navigator? If so, perhaps the course that had been plotted would have been more peaceful. I am not saying that with God at the helm you would not have troubled waters. Scripture is clear that we will have troubles and trials in this life. The point is, a good relationship with God will help you pass through rough waters. If you are able to see things from God's perspective, you can have a peace that passes all understanding and is not obtainable from any other source.

How would you feel about a situation wherein someone only approaches you when they want your help?

Jennings (Jay) Turner   2018

LET YOUR LIGHT SHINE
NUGGET 36

In the story of Lazarus, Mary and Martha (sisters of Lazarus) sent word to Jesus that Lazarus was sick. Jesus waited two days until Lazarus was dead before heading to Judaea where Lazarus was entombed. Martha went out and met him and said, "Jesus, Lord, if thou had been here, my brother would have not died." Jesus had already told his disciples that the sickness was "for the glory of God, that the Son of God might be glorified thereby." Jesus did raise Lazarus from the dead and in doing so was greatly glorified. He told Martha "I am the resurrection, and the life." In waiting until the situation was darker, the Lord's glory and authority were made clearer.

We are now waiting for the second coming of our Lord Jesus. Are not the times becoming darker all around us? God the Father will be glorified out of the darkness. The apostacy that is growing makes the world a darker place. How bright does your testimony burn today? We are the light of the world and the contrast should help with the harvest of lost souls. God will be greatly glorified at His coming. Let's glorify Him now with our lives and by loving others into the real church.

Jennings Turner   2018

LET JESUS WASH YOUR FEET
NUGGET 37

Please take a look at 1 Kings 6.19-20. Solomon was to build the temple for the habitation of the Lord. In the KJV this is referred to as the "oracle." This oracle is where the ark of the covenant of the Lord was to sit. This oracle (Holiest of Holies) was to be twenty cubits in length, twenty cubits in breadth, and twenty cubits in the height. This would make the oracle a cube just as we are told heaven is a cube. 1 Kings also tells us that the outer walls were the last thing to be built. That is to say, the resting place of God was built from the inside out.

One lesson from this is that no one should ever worry about cleaning up the outside, or the visible parts of their lives, before seeking God. Get it right on the inside before thinking about the outside. There is no amount or depth of sin or thought for which the blood of Jesus cannot atone. Salvation is clearly wholly of faith. You cannot add anything on your own to enhance your worthiness. God loves you personally so much that he gave us his only begotten Son, that whosoever believeth in him should not perish, but have everlasting life (John 3:16). He had to have his blood shed because only a perfect sacrifice could atone for our sins. His blood is sufficient for ANY sin. Turn toward God and seek him today.

Do you suppose that the inside of a healthy tree got that way because the outside looked wonderful? A healthy tree must have a healthy core first. Conversely, some trees look good on the outside but are dead and rotting on the inside. Just as in the instructions for building the temple, we must start with our inside. Are you spending more time on your outward appearance than your inner relationship with God?

Jennings (Jay) Turner   2018

EXERCISING FAITH CAN BE FRIGHTENING
NUGGET 38

Each year when I first start riding my bike, it takes some effort before my leg muscles (and rear) get toned enough to be comfortable. This seems to be true with almost any endeavor. This past winter, while staying in Florida, we were invited to try paddle boarding. My wife and I turned down several invitations before finally trying it. We figured we couldn't balance, were too old, etc. We were pretty shaky in the beginning but after trying it and sticking with it for a while, we gained confidence and we improved to where we enjoyed it.

I think that the examples above are good analogies as it relates to putting our faith into action. Most of us feel very insecure about being used by God. We have all kinds of doubts and excuses. However, Moses was eighty years of age when he was confronted with the burning bush. He didn't think he could speak clearly enough, he was afraid of confronting pharaoh, etc. Here is maybe the one thing to remember: if you feel inadequate for the task before you, that is more than likely a good thing. You see, that way you won't get in God's way. If you knew everything and how it would turn out, what role would faith play in anything? By its very nature, faith requires trust. Faith exercised is when something is put into motion based on trust. Hebrews 11.6 tells us that without faith it is impossible to please God.

If you feel led to step out in some way, do it. God has this. Just use common sense. I like to joke about my fifth-grade music teacher suggesting "Jay honey, just move your lips." Therefore, I am not going to be auditioning for a solo. Make sure it's not last night's pizza. One thing is for sure. We can all give our testimony and the gospel. Everyone has had an opportunity when they could have shared or been used by God in some way but kept still or silent. It happens. Sometimes success is getting up one more time than you have fallen. Go for it. You will never regret it in eternity.

Jennings (Jay) Turner   2018

RESPOND AS WHO YOU ARE
NUGGET 39

Please begin by looking at a few verses found in Ezekiel and taken from The Message. Ezekiel 20.8-9 reads, "But they rebelled against me, wouldn't listen to a word I said. None got rid of the vile things they were addicted to. They held on to the no-gods of Egypt as if for dear life. I seriously considered inflicting my anger on them in force right there in Egypt. Then I thought better of it. I acted out of who I was, not by how I felt. And if acted in a way that would evoke honor, not blasphemy, from the nations around them, nations who had seen me reveal myself by promising to lead my people out of Egypt."

In Ezekiel 20.14-16 (The Message), we read, "They didn't follow my statutes. They despised my laws for living well and obediently in the ways I had set out. And they totally desecrated my holy sabbaths. I seriously considered unleashing my anger on them right there in the desert. But I thought better of it and acted out of who I was, not by what I felt, so that I might be honored and not blasphemed by the nations who had seen me bring them out." Then again in 20.44, "But dear Israel, you'll also realize that I am God when I respond to you out of who I am, not by what I feel about the evil lives you've lived, the corrupt history you've compiled. Decree of God, the Master."

There is a lesson here for each of us. If we are children of God, we should allow His great love to manifest itself in our actions. We should not act out our feelings without considering the love that God wishes us to apply to others. Others (including Christians) are watching both our actions and speech and these are part of our testimony. The goal isn't to "look good" but rather to let the love of Jesus shine upon others. The tongue is truly in a slippery place! It is always best if the Holy Spirit is the filter for it.

Jennings (Jay) Turner   2018

WALK OR TALK
NUGGET 40

James 3:12 (KJV) says,"Can the fig tree, my brethren, bear olive berries? Either a vine, figs? so can no fountain both yield salt water and fresh." Notice that he is talking to "brethren." You can tell an apple tree by the fruit it bears. What is in your heart will eventually manifest itself in the fruit you bear; that is to say, your actions. In John 15:1(KJV) Jesus says,"I am the true vine, and my Father is the husbandman." Verse 4 in same chapter says,"Abide in me, and I in you. As the branch cannot bear fruit of itself, except it abide in the vine; no more can ye, except ye abide in me." From these verses we can conclude that if you wish to bring forth Godly fruit, you must abide in Christ. I also believe there is a practical application in these verses that we can apply in the world around us. If you are trying to discern another's intensions, pay more attention to their actions than their speech.

Jennings (Jay) Turner   2018

EXERCISE YOUR TALENTS
NUGGET 41

To paraphrase Matthew 25.14–30: To those servants who used their talents, he gave more – and took from those who did not.

I believe that as Christians (servants), if we look about us and make ourselves available, opportunities to love and serve others appear. True compassion requires contact and generally will involve some cost, whether it be our time, energy or even money. The Good Samaritan didn't just pray for the man in need. He didn't form a committee to evaluate the situation and suggest solutions. Have you known a Christian who often helps someone, even a stranger, with situations such as being stranded, out of gas, hungry, cold, etc.? I know a Christian that seems to encounter these "opportunities" regularly. Could it be that because he exercises his opportunities to love and serve others that God gives him even more opportunities? Perhaps God is giving him "my" or "your" opportunities because we passed them over. In the parable, the Master took from those not using their talents and gave them to the one exercising his talents.

God blessed us eternally through his son Jesus. We can bless him back by loving others as he clearly wishes us to do and being obedient to his word.

Jennings (Jay) Turner   2018

CROSS IN THE OLD TESTAMENT
NUGGET 42

In chapter 15 of Exodus, God's people have been in the wilderness three days without water. At Marah there was water but it was bitter. God showed Moses a tree and instructed him to cast it into the water. When this was accomplished, the water became sweet. Also, they were saved on the third day. This tree represented the cross that Jesus would eventually die upon. Check out these versus (KJV): Acts 5.30; "The God of our fathers raised up Jesus, whom ye slew and hanged on a tree." Acts 10.39; "And we are witnesses of all things which he did both in the land of the Jews, and in Jerusalem; whom they slew and hanged on a tree." Acts 13.29; "And when they had fulfilled all that was written of him, they took him down from the tree, and laid him in a sepulcher." And finally, Galatians 3.13; "Christ hath redeemed us from the curse of the law, being made a curse for us: it is written, Cursed is every one that hangeth on a tree." Marah and these bitter waters were directly in the path of God's people as they were being led to the promised land. The tree can be seen as a symbol of placing Christ in your life to help you with the bitterness of life.

The life and path of a Christian is not without many trials and tribulations. When you come to bitter and troubled waters in your life, try stirring them with the cross of Jesus. If you have ever trusted in Jesus, you have the Comforter (Holy Spirit) within you. You can have a joy that transcends circumstances.

Jennings (Jay) Turner.   2018

I CAN TAKE IT FROM HERE
NUGGET 43

Read Joshua 24. Just before his death, Joshua recounted the many blessings of God. God had delivered all the tribes that had inhabited Canaan into the hands of the Israelites. Israel dwelt in cities they had not built. They had vineyards and orchards they had not planted. God had greatly blessed them. Yet, given time, God's people began to go in a direction they thought to be preferable. I wonder if over time they began to believe that it was through their own efforts and prowess that they were living in such a wonderful situation. Maybe the thought of some was "thanks for the boost, but we can take it from here."

Is this not a danger for us today? Have you ever had a self-satisfying thought of "look what I have accomplished or accumulated?" Or, "I have both earned and deserve this secure existence?" It is far better for us to keep a tight grip on God's hand, thank him for his blessings, and take the next step he reveals to us. Our country, in many ways, has turned from God. How does that seem to be working out?

Jennings (Jay) Turner   2018

DON'T KEEP ONE FOOT IN THE WORLD
NUGGET 44

In Exodus, Egypt represents the world and Pharaoh represents Satan. God chose Moses to lead his people out of Egypt and their slavery. God was with Moses and gave him specific instructions along each step of the way. When Pharaoh would not let God's people leave, judgments were imposed on Egypt. At first, Pharaoh said the Jews could worship in the land (world). Moses refused because God's instructions were that everything and everyone were to leave. Next, they could worship in the wilderness but they were not to go far. Next, some could go but not their young nor could they take any animals, etc., etc. Finally, the Egyptians paid them to go. The point here is that Satan desires to keep you in the world, but if he can't keep you immersed in the world, he will try to compromise you into staying as close as possible. These tactics are still in use on us today. Be aware. Don't compromise.

Jennings (Jay) Turner   2018

GIVE TO GOD FIRST
NUGGET 45

Read 1 Kings 17.8-24. Here, Elijah is told to dwell at Zarephath where a widow with a son will sustain him. Elijah asks for food and the widow says she has only a handful of meal in a barrel and a little oil in a cruse and that she is about to prepare this last bit so that she and her son will not starve. Elijah responds, "Fear not, go as you say but make me a little cake first, bring it to me, then prepare meal for yourself and your son." The widow was told that neither the meal or oil would fail until the famine was over. She believed and prepared Elijah a cake. The word of God, spoken through Elijah, was true and neither the meal nor the oil failed.

There is an old story or song about a man dying of thirst who comes upon an old pump. He pumps but no water comes out. He sees a note attached to a small canteen. The note says there is a little water in the canteen to drink but it would be far better to pour the water down the pump, thereby priming it by wetting the leather valve. The man is caught in a quandary. He can get some immediate gratification, or, exercising some faith, pour the water down and possibly receive much more in the future. The metaphor is clear.

The widow gave to God first.

Jennings (Jay) Turner   2018

UNASHAMED PURSUIT WITH LOVE
NUGGET 46

In the book of Hosea, the prophet is told by God that he is to find a whore and marry her. She is to be the mother of his children. Hosea picked Gomer and she became his wife. God told Hosea that the reason for his instructions was because the entire country of Israel had become a whorehouse and unfaithful. Gomer continued to seek other lovers but when things went very badly for her, she always returned to Hosea. She bore Hosea children. Throughout all this, Hosea had no shame admitting to the world that he loved his wife passionately and that it broke his heart when she went back to prostitution. When she was broken and hungry and had to sell herself as a slave, he bought her back (paraphrased from *The Message*).

All throughout the word we see over and over again where God's people have been delivered from destruction and blessed but again and again they return to their no-gods and blatant, rebellious sinning. As we read, it often seems hard to believe that God's people don't reside where they are blessed but turn away from him. When they go their own way, it always turns out badly. Yet, don't we keep making the same mistake ourselves? How many times have *we* put something or someone before our savior? As with Hosea and Gomer, God never stops loving us and pursuing us. He loves us unconditionally. When we turn toward him, his arms are always ready to receive us. Think of how we grieve God when we turn away. We all need to focus on running after him. It is the surest way to have a fulfilled life.

Jennings (Jay) Turner   2018

ARE YOU HAND IN HAND WITH GOD?
NUGGET 47

In the KJV, Amos 3.3 says, "Can two walk together, except they be agreed?" The same verse in The Message reads, "Do two people walk hand in hand if they aren't going to the same place?" Therefore, if you place your hand in God's, you will be headed in His direction. God is not only your creator but he has proven his amazing love for you by sending his only son to be a sacrifice for the sins of the world. Therefore, will he not lead you to a place of peace, security and everlasting life?

Jennings (Jay) Turner   2018

GOD IS KNOCKING
NUGGET 48

Revelation 3.20 says that Jesus stands at your door and knocks (Jesus). He will not barge in. Luke 14.7–11 says that he will not sit at the head of your table (the throne of your heart) unless you invite him there. Also, we are told that if you are invited to a wedding, you should not take a place in the highest room (place of honor) unless you are bidden to go there. As much as God loves us, he will not force himself upon any of us. If you make the decision to turn toward him and place your hand in his, we are told that there is much rejoicing in heaven. Literally, what on earth could you be waiting for?

Jennings (Jay) Turner   2018

DWELLING ON THE WORLD
NUGGET 49

Genesis 13.10-12 says: "And Lot lifted up his eyes, and beheld all the plain of Jordan, that it was well watered every where, before the Lord destroyed Sodom and Gomorrah, even as the garden of the Lord, like the land of Egypt, as thou comest unto Zoar. Then Lot chose him all the plain of Jordan; and Lot journeyed east: and they separated themselves the one from the other. Abram dwelled in the land of Canaan, and Lot dwelled in the cities of the plain, and pitched his tent toward Sodom."

By pitching his tent toward Sodom, Lot was continually taking in worldly Sodom and the sin with which it was infested. Before long, Lot had backslidden and was down in Sodom. This is a warning to us. We need to keep guard that we do not spend too much time dwelling on the things of the world. I once heard it said that you can't be blamed for having a bird land on your head but, then again, you shouldn't let it build a nest there. Please, pitch your tent in the direction of the Lord.

Jennings (Jay) Turner

WHO'S YOUR NEIGHBOR?
NUGGET 50

In Mark 12:29-31, Jesus tells us that the first of all the commandments is that we love the Lord our God with all our heart, with all our soul, with all our mind, and with all our strength. He then adds that the second is that we love our neighbors as ourselves. Jesus says that these two trump all other commandments. In Luke 10:25-37 we have the story of a lawyer who questioned Jesus. The lawyer wants to know what he must do to inherit eternal life. Jesus asked him "What is written in the law?" The lawyer answered by quoting the above two commandments. Jesus confirmed this is correct, but the lawyer, wanting to justify himself, asked "Who is my neighbor?" Jesus answered him by telling the parable of the good Samaritan. At the end of the parable, Jesus asked him who he believed was a neighbor to the fallen man. The answer was "he who had mercy on him."

So, who is our neighbor? I think the parable indicates it is anyone in need of mercy. Anyone to whom we can be of help. If we know the gospel, then we know the cure for sin. Given an opportunity to share this good news, we should be a good neighbor and share it. People in need of mercy generally require contact from us, not just prayers.

Each of us is called to do more than just wave to a neighbor. I have some neighbors that are nearly strangers. We should pray for each other to gain boldness.

Jennings (Jay) Turner   2018

LEADERS SHOULD LISTEN TO GOD
NUGGET 51

In 2 Samuel chapter 24, King David decides to number the people of his kingdom. He is warned that he is not to proceed with the numbering but, we are told, he delighted in numbering the people and gave orders for the numbering to begin. God's anger is kindled and although it is David's sin, all Israel suffers. God sent a pestilence that took the lives of seventy-thousand men. All leaders should be careful to be sure that the path they are trying to take others on is not for personal gratification. Wrong paths usually have warning signs.

Jennings (Jay) Turner   2018

GRACE FROM GOD, JUSTICE WITH MEN
NUGGET 52

Have you ever had an acquaintance or co-worker, or known of a political figure who has taken advantage of others for personal gain? Perhaps this person's actions have even been illegal. I would guess that most of us have experienced or are at least aware of such behavior. I certainly have and it usually causes me to feel outrage. Leviticus 19:36 says, "Just balances, just weights, a just ephah, and a just hin, shall ye have: I am the Lord your God, which brought you out of the land of Egypt." We know that God wants us to pursue justice and show mercy here on earth. There can be a temptation here in the flesh to wish some individuals to receive punishment (justice instead of grace) at the hand of God at the Great White Throne judgment.

1 Timothy 1:15 tells us that Jesus came into the world to save sinners. Therefore, according to 1 Timothy 2, we are to make supplications, prayers, and intercessions for all men. This isn't optional. In Job 31 scripture also says that we are not to rejoice at the destruction of those who hate us nor rejoice if evil should find them.

No saved person would ever wish to receive justice from God. We wish to receive his *grace* through faith in his son Jesus. Whatever wrongs someone has committed, our desire, prayers and supplications should be that they will repent and find God through a right relationship with Jesus Christ. If that happens, not only would you lose an adversary, you would gain a brother or sister in Christ.

In the Lord's prayer doesn't it say, "Forgive us our trespasses as we forgive those who trespass against us?" Hopefully, those words haven't been spoken so many times that we are somewhat numb to the underlying meaning. We are actually praying that God will forgive *us* as *we* forgive others. This realization is a real motivator for me. I may help bring someone to justice, but I should also forgive him. Whenever the opportunity presents itself, share the gospel with love.

Jennings (Jay) Turner   2018

RESURRECTION KNOWN LONG AGO
NUGGET 53

Resurrection is not only a New Testament phenomenon. Consider the following examples.

In the first 23 verses of 2 Samuel chapter 12 we read about the consequences that came upon David as a result of him desiring to have the wife of Uriah. Earlier, David had seen Uriah's wife, Bathsheba, bathing on a rooftop and desired her. He, in fact, had relations with her and she became pregnant. Uriah was a soldier and was away in battle such that he could not be the father. David called Uriah back from battle in hopes that Uriah would believe he was the father. However, Uriah was so honorable that he would not lie with his wife since his fellow soldiers were still in battle. Therefore, David ordered that Uriah be sent into the most heated area in the battle so that he might be killed. Uriah was killed and then David took Bathsheba to be his wife. God was angered and sent the prophet Nathan to David to confront him. Part of the punishment for David was that the child that had resulted would die. The child did not die for seven days. During that time, David wept, fasted and slept on the earth. He would not respond to any questions from the servants. After the child died, David arose from the ground, washed, anointed himself, put on clean clothes, worshipped, and went and ate. His servants asked him why the change. He replied, "While the child was alive, I fasted and wept: for I said, Who can tell whether God will be gracious to me, that the child may live? But now he is dead, wherefore should I fast? Can I bring him back again? I shall go to him, but he shall not return to me." David was confident that he would see his dead son again. David believed in the resurrection. David shows us that sometimes we need to take the "long view" rather than focus on the immediate situation.

Jennings (Jay) Turner   2018

FIRST SALVATION, THEN WORKS
NUGGET 54

We know from scriptures that we cannot be saved by works (Ephesians 2-8-9). Works you have done in the flesh do not count toward salvation. Salvation comes before meaningful works. In Luke 7:50, Jesus tells a woman, "Thy faith hath saved thee; go in peace." Read also 2 Timothy 1:9 wherein, Paul, referring to our Lord, says, "Who hath saved us, and called us with a holy calling, not according to our works, but according to his own purpose and grace, which was given us in Christ Jesus before the world began." First, accept salvation. This is a free gift paid for with the blood sacrifice of Jesus. The woman in Luke 7 is saved by her faith, not works. Salvation makes you safe from the penalty of sin. When saved, you become a cell in the body of Christ, which is the church. The Holy Spirit will indwell you and will begin a work in every aspect of your life. Read Matthew 3.11 where John the Baptist says, "I'm baptizing you here in the river, turning your old life in for a kingdom life. The real action comes next: The main character in this drama–compared to him I'm a mere stagehand–will ignite the kingdom life within you, a fire within you, the Holy Spirit within you, changing you from the inside out (from The Message)."

At this point, God is able to work through you. In The Message, Romans 11:7 reads, "The chosen ones of God (the elect) were those who let God pursue his interest in them, and as a result received his stamp of legitimacy." Worded another way, when we allow the Holy Spirit to be on the throne of our lives, we will become more like Christ and he is able to use us according to his will.

Jennings (Jay) Turner   2018

FAITH, LOVE AND HOPE
NUGGET 55

Faith inspires works
Love prompts obedience
Hope produces joy and peace that helps us to endure

Saving faith means that the Holy Spirit resides in you. When yielded to the Holy Spirit, God can use you as an implement for *his* purpose.

Love evokes the desire to please: not from duty but from the heart. To bless a loved one is love in motion.

The hope that lies within a Christian brings a peace that passes all understanding. Troubles in this life come to all of us but the more we grow spiritually, the more we are able to get a glimpse of life from God's perspective and this is a comfort when things in the world are troubling.

Jennings (Jay) Turner   2018

GOD AND MAMMON
NUGGET 56

In Luke 16.13 KJV we are told that we cannot serve both God and mammon (the world). Notice the word "serve". You can have only one master.

In Mark 10.21-22 KJV we see the story of the rich young ruler. Jesus told him to sell his possessions and follow him but the rich young man was sad and went away grieved for he had great possessions.

It is okay for us to have many things but it is not okay if we put anything before God. Seek first the kingdom of God.

Money makes a great servant but a terrible master.

God gave us people to love and things to use, but if we love things, we will use people.

Jennings (Jay) Turner   2018

THE YOKE'S ON YOU
NUGGET 57

When I think of a yoke, I envision a pair of oxen yoked together. I assume that they learn to work in unison. If they were each trying to go their own way I can imagine the strain on their entire being and the chaffing on their necks.

In Matt 11.29-30 Jesus implores us to take his yoke upon us so that we may find rest in our souls. In Gal 5.1 we are told that Christ has made us free so as not to be entangled again with the yoke of bondage.

Even after we have, by faith, yoked ourselves to Jesus, don't we at times try to go our own way? In the end, doesn't this decision also strain our very being? Read Ps 32.1-9. In the first two verses we know that God is addressing those whose transgressions have been forgiven. Verse 8 indicates that God desires to guide these people with his eye. In verse 9 he warns us to not be like a horse or mule who must be guided with bit and bridle.

If by faith you have taken on the yoke of Jesus, always seek his way. His way leads to a joyous and full life. If you do so, you are still yoked. You must still pick up and bear your on cross but you will be blessed in both your journey and your destination.

Jennings (Jay) Turner   2018

THE BIBLE IS A PERSONAL LETTER
NUGGET 58

When you sit down to read your bible, don't approach it as something abstract. Sure, the Bible covers many, many generations and topics but it is a letter meant to be personal to each of us.

All of the admonitions, lessons and stories are directly relevant to each of us today. At the center of the Bible is not man but God in three persons. God has pursued us since the fall of man in the garden of Eden. He has pursued us with a holy vigor that led him to sacrifice his only begotten Son to provide us with an avenue of reconciliation.

When you look into your bible, please know that it is a personal letter from our creator himself. Read it as such, yield yourself to its study and the blessings are beyond what you think possible.

Jennings (Jay) Turner   2018

SOME TROUBLES HELP US GROW
NUGGET 59

Job 42.6 KJV reads: "Wherefore I abhor myself, and repent in dust and ashes." In the Scofield Bible, a portion of the footnote for this verse reads; "The godly are afflicted that they may be brought to self-knowledge and self-judgment. Such afflictions are not penal for their sins, but remedial and purifying."

Have you ever gone through a trial of some sort and afterwards looked back and realized that during that period you were drawn closer to God and maybe matured somewhat in your christian walk? I have experienced this phenomenon.

Sometimes obstacles and hurdles are opportunities for growth. You don't have to get through these situations on your own. We, the Church, should always be looking for opportunities to help our brothers and sisters through difficulties. The Christian army has been known to shoot their own wounded. A priority of the Church (body of believers) is to reach out in love to everyone and anyone we can.

Jennings (Jay) Turner   2018

GLORIFYING GOD
NUGGET 60

Martha, upset with Jesus because her brother died before Jesus arrived, said: "Lazarus would not have died had you been here." Jesus waited so that God would be glorified when he raised Lazarus from the dead.

Why is Jesus waiting now while the world ripens with apostacy? Perhaps it is because the Father will be glorified out of the darkness. We should be glorifying God NOW with our lives.

Jennings (Jay) Turner   2018

TAKE UP YOUR CROSS
NUGGET 61

In Matthew 16.24, Jesus tells his disciples, "If any man will come after me, let him deny himself, and take up his cross, and follow me." I am sure that "taking up your cross" can be looked at in many ways. I believe that one of those ways is simply that you lay down anything and everything that can hinder you from following Jesus.

If we desire to follow after our savior, each of us surely knows when we are encountering something that is best avoided. If in doubt, ask the Holy Spirit to help guide you. Doesn't it seem reasonable that the more you put down, the easier it will be to carry your cross?

Jennings (Jay) Turner   2018

THE LIGHT WHEN JESUS RETURNS
NUGGET 62

At the return of Jesus, the light will be so bright (like an X-ray) all darkness will be seen in the light of his holiness. Nothing will be hidden. All sin will be exposed. All knees will bow.

To be face to face with the holy God will be terrifying enough that the scripture says some will try to end their lives. We get a sense of this in Mark chapter four when Jesus is asleep in the back of the boat during a ferocious storm while the disciples, in the front of the boat, are certain that they will perish. A disciple then awoke Jesus and asked him, "care ye not that we perish?" Then, when Jesus rebuffed them for their lack of faith, he calmed the sea. Scripture then says that the disciples were more fearful of the holiness and power of Jesus than they had been when they believed they would perish. Revelation tells us that at the second coming of Jesus, many will desire the rocks to fall upon them. Same fear?

Jennings (Jay) Turner   2019

WATCH FOR "TYPES"
NUGGET 63

1. Abraham was a type of the Father, who spared not His own son, but delivered Him up for us all (John 3.16). He was also a type of King who seeks a bride for His son.

2. Sarah (God changed her name from Sarai) became a mother of nations. She was a freewoman and represented Israel.

3. Hagar was a bondwoman under the law who gave birth to Ishmael. She was subject to Sarah but used the natural birth of Ismael to cause Sarah distress.

4. Ishmael was a "natural" son, born because of unbelief on the part of Abraham and Sarah. God had told Sarah that she would bare a son but she doubted because she was well on in years. She suggested to Abraham that he take her handmaid Hagar for a wife. Hagar became pregnant and Ishmael was born.

5. Isaac was a type of Christ. He was a "spiritual" child born to Sarah who was very old. In chapter 22 of Genesis, God tested Abraham. He told Abraham to take his "only son" (his only spiritual son) and offer him for a burnt-offering. Isaac was not a child, yet, he willingly carried the wood for his own sacrifice and obeyed his father. Jesus also obeyed the will of his father and also carried the wood (cross) for his own sacrifice.

When Abraham stretched forth the knife to slay Isaac, an angel of the Lord stopped him, and when Abraham looked up, a ram was caught by its horns in a thicket. In Genesis 22:8 Abraham stated that God would provide himself a lamb for a burnt-offering. I don't believe it was a play on words when he said "God will provide himself." When God sent us Jesus, he in fact provided himself as a sacrifice. Praise Him forever.

The natural son, Ishmael, is sent off and rejected. The spiritual son, Isaac, is accepted and carries the promise. All of the above happens in chapter 22 of Genesis. Immediately after chapter 22 Israel (Sarah) dies. Then in chapter 24, Abraham tells his servant, an unnamed servant who rules over all that he has, to seek a bride for his son Isaac. This unnamed servant (Eleazer?) must represent the Holy Spirit. He calls no attention to himself, goes out to seek a bride for the Son. This Servant points the bride at the Son. Through His testimony, the bride is deeply in love with the Son even without laying eyes on Him. Take a look at 1 Peter 1:9. In the KJV it reads: "Whom having not seen, ye love; in whom, though now ye see him not, yet believing, ye rejoice with joy unspeakable and full of glory."

Examples of these "types" appear repeatedly in scripture. For example, when reading about Joseph, do you identify him as being a type of Christ? Joseph was rejected by his brethren. He was sold for a price. His brethren believed they had killed him when they left him in the ground. Joseph is "resurrected" from the pit after three days. Joseph is exalted by the Gentiles. Joseph, after being rejected by his brethren (the sons of Jacob who is also known as Israel), takes a bride from the Gentiles. He then makes himself known to his brethren and reconciles them to his father. Whether reading in the Old or New Testaments these "types" can be found. The fact that these all tie together is a real "faith builder" in my walk. I pray that these will also be a blessing to you.

Jennings (Jay) Turner   2019

GODLY CHASTISEMENT
NUGGET 64

Hebrews 12:7-11 NIV: 7) "Endure hardship as discipline; God is treating you as sons. For what son is not disciplined by his father? 8) If you are not disciplined, and everyone undergoes discipline, then you are illegitimate children and not true sons. 9) Moreover, we have all had human fathers who disciplined us and we respected them for it. How much more should we submit to the Father of our spirits and live! 10) Our fathers disciplined us for a little while as they thought best; but God disciplines us for our good, that we may share in his holiness. 11) No discipline seems pleasant at the time, but painful. Later on, however, it produces a harvest of righteousness and peace for those who have been trained by it."

The following quote was taken from a footnote in the Scofield bible in reference to Job:42-6:

"The godly are afflicted that they may be brought to self-knowledge and self-judgment. Such afflictions are not penal (punishment) for their sins, but remedial and purifying".

Jennings (Jay) Turner   2019

LAW AND GRACE CONTRASTS
NUGGET 65

The goal of this nugget is to show a few of the contrasts between Law and Grace. In presenting these contrasts, I would not wish anyone to think that the Law (Moses and the commandments) is bad. Romans 3:19-20 KJV reads, "Now we know that whatever the law says, it says to those who are under the law, that every mouth may be stopped, and all the world may become guilty before God. Therefore by the deeds of the law no flesh will be justified in His sight, for by the law is the knowledge of sin." This does not mean that the Law is bad. In Matthew 5:17 Jesus says: "Do not think that I came to destroy the Law or the Prophets. I did not come to destroy but to fulfill." In 2 Timothy 3:16-17 we are told "All scripture is given by inspiration of God, and is profitable for doctrine, for reproof, for correction, for instruction in righteousness, that the man of God may be complete, thoroughly equipped for every good work."

Under LAW: Do and live.

Under GRACE: Believe and live.

Under LAW: Abel's blood called out for justice.

Under GRACE: The blood of Jesus calls out for forgiveness for anyone who believes upon Him.

Under LAW: When Moses first brought the law down from Mount Sinai, three thousand died. (Ex 32:28)

Under GRACE: On the day of Pentecost (Acts 2:41), when Peter first preached the gospel, three thousand were saved.

Under LAW: In the parable of the Good Samaritan (Luke 10:30-37), a Levite, who represents the Law, passes by the dying man and leaves him as he was.

Under GRACE: The Samaritan, a type of Christ, had compassion on the dying man. He went to him, bandaged his wounds, poured on oil and wine; and he set him on his own animal, brought him to an inn, and took care of him. He also promised to return again. I say the Samaritan "was a type of christ" because of the following: Samaritans were rejected by their brethren. He attended to the wounds the world had imparted upon the dying man. He poured on oil, a symbol of the Holy Spirit and wine, which is a symbol of blood. He then put the dying man in *his* place, then provided a place of rest that *he* paid for and then promised to return again. That is grace.

Under LAW: Sheep were sacrificed for the Shepherd.

Under GRACE: The Great Shepherd became a willing sacrifice for the sheep. Greater grace cannot be imagined. Praises forever!

Jennings (Jay) Turner

DON'T PUT BRACES ON BABY TEETH
NUGGET 66

I have never seen a baby wearing braces. The reason is simple. Their baby teeth are not their permanent teeth. The analogy is straight forward. If you have been saved, you are in this world, but not of this world. In spite of this, aren't we pulled to the things that the world tells us will satisfy us? The only thing that will truly satisfy our inner soul is a personal relationship with God through his Son Jesus. Having things isn't the problem. The problem comes if we love them and seek them first above the kingdom of God. God is love and He commands us to love Him with all our heart and to also love one another and our neighbors as ourselves. There is a wonderful peace promised to anyone who will but seek it. Philippians 4:6-7 (KJV) reads: "Be careful for nothing; but in every thing by prayer and supplication with thanksgiving let your requests be made known to God. And the peace of God, which passeth all understanding, shall keep your hearts and minds through Christ Jesus."

James 4:14 tells us that our life is as a vapor that appears but for a little time before it vanishes.

1 Timothy 6:17-19 (KJV); "Charge them that are rich in this world, that they be not high-minded, nor trust in uncertain riches, but in the living God, who giveth us richly all things to enjoy; That they do good, that they be rich in good works, ready to distribute, willing to communicate; Laying up in store for themselves a good foundation against the time to come, that they may lay hold on eternal life."

Finally, consider the eternal impact of 1 Timothy 6:7 (KJV); "For we brought nothing into this world and it is certain we can carry nothing out". In light of this, isn't focusing on the cares of this world like putting braces on baby teeth? We should each be most concerned about our eternal home.

Jennings (Jay) Turner   2019

DON'T GO TO THE WORLD FOR HELP AND COMFORT
NUGGET 67

When God's people are tested, there is a temptation to turn to the world for help and comfort. In Genesis 12:10 we see that a great famine had come into the land and Abram (not yet Abraham) took Sarai (not yet Sarah), his wife and went into Egypt. In the Bible, Egypt is synonymous with the World. They even entered Egypt with a lie. That is, Abram told Sarai to tell anyone they encountered that she was his sister; not his wife. There was eventually a terrible price to be paid for turning to Egypt instead of God.

Turning to the World when facing problems might yield short-term relief but may also yield long-term consequences. God always knows what we are experiencing. He loves us with a perfect love. Trust Him. Have faith and rely on Him for a present and eternal solution.

Jennings (Jay) H. Turner   2019

GUARD YOUR TESTIMONY
NUGGET 68

In chapter thirteen of Genesis we find Abram (soon to be Abraham) and Lot traveling together. Between them, they possessed such a quantity of flocks, and herds, and tents that the land was not able to bear them. Their substance was so great that they were no longer able to dwell together. The situation required them to part. Abram, so as to keep and promote peace between them, offered to let Lot choose the land and way he wished to go. Therefore, Lot eyed all the land before them and chose for himself what he believed to be the best. This was Lot's first step into backsliding. His eyes beheld something he wanted and he put himself first in order to pursue it. Next, Lot dwelled in the cities of the plain, and pitched his tent toward Sodom. By pitching his tent in this way, it allowed Lot to continually dwell upon Sodom. The men of Sodom were wicked before the Lord exceedingly. This was his second step.

In the beginning of chapter nineteen of Genesis we see that Lot has taken the third step in his backsliding. He is now a great man in Sodom and sits in the city gate. Two angels came to Lot and informed him that they had been sent to remove him and his family out of Sodom before its destruction. Lot spoke to his sons-in-law exhorting them to come with him out of Sodom before its was too late. His sons-in-law would not listen to him. He finally accompanied the angels out of Sodom with his wife and two daughters. If you will read 2 Peter 2:7&8 you will see that Lot was a just man. God had mercy on him. The angels warned that, now that they were removed from Sodom, they were not to look back. Lot's wife did look back and she became a pillar of salt.

I have suffered from not adhering to some of the lessons in this story. I hope we can all learn something from this. Lot chose for himself things that would yield a current advantage. Abraham looked for a city with its foundation based upon God (Hebrews 10:11). Lot pitched his tent toward Sodom. That is, he began to look and dwell upon inappropriate things. The next thing he knew, he was living in it. Living among and partaking in the sin cost Lot most of the saltiness of his testimony. In the end, his sons-in-law would not listen because they thought he was mocking them. They could no longer take him seriously. Matthew 5:13 says that the saved are the salt of the earth, but if salt has lost its taste (strength and quality) how can its saltiness be restored? Could this be why when Lot's wife looked back she became a pillar of salt? Keeping our eyes and thoughts on eternal things and seeking the advice of God and fellow believers will go a long way to keeping us headed in the proper direction.

Jennings (Jay) H. Turner   2019

APPLY THE BLOOD
NUGGET 69

The blood of a sacrifice has always been required by God in order to cover sin. In the Garden of Eden, after Adam and Eve had sinned, they covered themselves with leaves. Leaves were not sufficient. God made them coats of skins and covered Adam and Eve with them. A blood sacrifice happened in order to provide skins. Later, we see the offerings of Cain and Abel to the Lord. Cain was a tiller of the ground and offered the first fruits of his crop. It was unacceptable. Abel was a keeper of sheep and so offered to the Lord the firstlings of his flock and the fat thereof. The sacrificed sheep were accepted.

God tested Abraham by instructing him to take his only son Isaac and to sacrifice him. Abraham had already told Isaac that God would provide Himself a lamb. Just as Abraham was about to slay his son, God told him to stop. When Abraham looked up, he saw a ram caught with its horns caught in a thicket. This lamb was then slain and offered up as an offering. This is a picture of what Jesus would do for us.

When God delivered His people out of Egypt, the final plague on Pharaoh and Egypt was the death of the firstborn. God instructed Moses and Aaron to tell the entire congregation to take a male lamb without blemish (a picture of Jesus) and slay it. The blood, by faith was to be struck upon the side posts and upper post of the door. God promised that when He saw the blood, He would pass over that house (hence "Passover"). Again, blood was required to avoid judgment.

There are many examples of blood being used (sometimes sprinkled) for atonement of sin in the Bible. Let us look at one more before considering the sacrifice of Jesus. The Ark of the Covenant was kept in the "Holiest of Holies" in the tabernacle. Once a year the high priest would enter and pour blood upon the top of the ark. One of the three items contained in the ark was the broken tablets of God's law. It seems to me that, this way, when God looked down upon His broken law, He saw it through the blood.

None of the above mentioned type of sacrifices could result in a permanent covering of sin but God so loved us that He sent His only begotten Son to be a perfect sacrifice for sins. Jesus, who knew no sin, became sin so that He could be a worthy and permanent sacrifice for us. Therefore, I implore you, by faith, to apply the blood of Jesus to the doorposts of your heart. By doing so, God will see your sins through the blood of Jesus. During the Passover, God skipped over the homes who, by faith, had applied blood to their doorposts. He did not skip over homes based on the works of those inside. It was the blood.

Do you yearn to be reconciled to God? Do you have a desire to follow and emulate Jesus? Do you regret your past sins? If so, this is called repentance. Will you sin again? Of course. If you desire forgiveness and salvation, call upon Him.

Jennings (Jay) Turner   2019

DANGER IN HANGING ON TO THE WORLD
NUGGET 70

I once watched a wildlife show that showed a man trying to catch monkeys. The technique he employed was very interesting and seemed to me to be an example or analogy that can apply to each of us. The filming took place in a location that consisted of a very large abandoned ant hill surrounded by trees inhabited by monkeys. The ant hill appeared to be about six feet in height and about four feet in diameter. It appeared to have dried so that the outside was very hard. The man trying to catch monkeys began by making some holes through the exterior of the ant hill that each had a specific circumference. Inside each hole, he made a small pocket. Next, he removed some shiny metal balls that appeared to be ball bearings. He then proceeded to juggle the shiny balls in front of the monkeys. Next, he placed one ball into each hole he had made. He then withdrew from the ant hill and waited. Some of the monkeys then approached the ant hill and reached into the holes to retrieve a ball. The holes had been sized so that if a monkey clenched a ball with its fist, it could not remove its hand without letting go of the ball. The monkeys must have highly prized the shiny balls because they would not let go of the ball thereby trapping themselves. They were then captured.

One possible analogy seemed very clear to me. The world we live in has many shiny balls that attract us. If any of these "shiny balls" interfere with seeking a relationship with God, we must be willing to let go. I believe that possessing some "shiny balls" is fine as long as none of them is making us subject to being captured by the world.

Jennings (Jay) Turner   2019

- 83 -

DO GOOD WORKS IN SECRET
NUGGET 71

We tend to think of rewards in worldly terms. We should not perform good deeds in order to receive recognition from others around us. Matthew 6:1 (KJV) says, "Take heed that ye do not your alms before men, to be seen of them: otherwise ye have no reward of your Father which is in heaven."

Let's all try the following exercise: 1. Pray for an opportunity; 2. Don't get in God's way. Allow him to use you. 3. Don't try to get any recognition for what is accomplished. He says that he will see what you do in secret. Just allow yourself to be used by God as a way of blessing him. God blessed us eternally through his son Jesus. We can bless him back by loving others as he clearly wishes us to do and being obedient to his word.

Jennings (Jay) Turner   2019

GOD IS PATIENT AND MERCIFUL
NUGGET 72

The story of the oldest man recorded in the Bible is found in chapter 5 of Genesis. It is Methuselah, a son of Enoch. The name "Methuselah" means "when he dies the judgment will come." God is long-suffering with us. I believe that because judgment was to come when Methuselah died, it is not a coincidence that he was the oldest man.

When a person is dying, the last thing that usually shuts down is the hearing. I believe this may be another example of the patience and mercy that God shows us. Romans 10.17 KJV reads "So then faith cometh by hearing, and hearing by the word of God."

Praise Him for His great love.

Jennings (Jay) Turner   2019

CORNELIUS AND THE GOSPEL
NUGGET 73

When studying the Bible, it is a blessing when it is revealed to you how something in one part of scripture relates so perfectly to another. Those experiences help to build and strengthen our faith. An example is when reading the account of Cornelius in Acts chapter 10. An angel appears to him and tells him to send for Peter, who will tell him how to be saved. The angel tells Cornelius that Peter is in Joppa. Sending people to Joppa and bringing Peter back could not have been a small task. I wondered why the angel didn't just tell Cornelius the gospel. It was much later when a bell rang when reading I Thessalonians 2.4. In that verse it says that we (the saved) were allowed of God to be put in trust with the gospel. The angel could not share the gospel. Sharing the gospel is our privilege and responsibility. When a question gets answered, it is a blessing. Be patient while mining those Bible nuggets.

Jennings (Jay) Turner.   2019

DO NOT GLEAN THE FIELD
NUGGET 74

———————— ❈ ————————

Leviticus 19.9-10 KJV reads: "And when ye reap the harvest of your land, thou shalt not wholly reap the corners of thy field, neither shalt thou gather the gleanings of thy harvest. And thou shalt not glean thy vineyard, neither shalt thou gather every grape of thy vineyard; thou shalt leave them for the poor and stranger: I am the Lord your God."

Does this infer that those in need, if able, are responsible to work for their need? An alternative would be for the land owner to harvest everything and then simply hand it out to those in need.

Certainly some people would not be able to enter the fields but I think the implication here is that everyone should do what they can. This cannot, however, blunt our love and service to everyone. May Holy discernment help us all.

Jennings (Jay) Turner   2019

DO NOT ASSIMILATE INTO APOSTATE SOCIETY
NUGGET 75

One of the great messages of the book of Revelation is that God reins. He was in charge from the beginning, still is, and will always be. Revelation 1.8 says: "I am Alpha and Omega, the beginning and the ending, saith the Lord, which is, and which was, and which is to come, the Almighty." We know how it ends in complete victory for God's people. We are admonished to stand firm and trust even when we face persecution or are surrounded by apostasy. One thing for sure is that if society is moving away from God, we are not to assimilate ourselves into the movement. We should not be complacent.

Jeremiah 51.1(KJV): "Thus saith the Lord; Behold, I will raise up against Babylon, and against them that dwell in the midst of them that rise up against me, a destroying wind."

Ezekiel 9.4-6(KJV): "And the Lord said unto him, Go through the midst of the city, through the midst of Jerusalem, and set a mark upon the foreheads of the men that sigh and that cry for all the abominations that be done in the midst thereof. And to the others he said in mine hearing, Go ye after him through the city and smite: let not your eye spare, neither have ye pity: Slay utterly old and young, both maids, and little children and women: but come not near any man upon whom is the mark; and begin at my sanctuary. Then they began at the ancient men which were before the house."

Share the gospel, oppose apostasy, and stand firm in your faith and trust God...........because God has this. If you are saved, you are in this world but you are not of this world. Others should be able to notice.

Jennings (Jay) Turner   2019

LESSON FROM HABAKKUK
NUGGET 76

In chapters 1 and 2 of Habakkuk we see that the prophet is questioning God about the iniquity and violence that surrounds God's people and why God has not seemingly addressed it. I think that this shows that it is okay to question God but we need to have the attitude of Habakkuk when waiting for an answer.

The prophet says that he will patiently watch to see what God will say to him and what he will answer when he is reproved. Habakkuk is willing and diligent to listen and he accepts that God is holy and correct. Although he doesn't understand why God is not yet dealing with the sin and violence surrounding him, he has faith that it is his understanding that is deficient and that in due time the perfect will of God will be revealed. When he is reproved, he welcomes it as a way to grow and understand.

Let us realize, as we see the sin all around us, that God's will and timing is perfect and beyond our discernment. We need to be patient, hold fast to our faith, proclaim the gospel, and know that God is in control.

Jennings (Jay) Turner   2019

JONAH RUNNING TO GOD
NUGGET 77

The book of Jonah only has four chapters. I have seen them depicted as follows: chapter 1 = Jonah running from God; chapter 2 = Jonah running to God; chapter 3 = Jonah running with God; and finally, chapter 4 = Jonah running ahead of God.

In one respect Jonah could be said to be a fore shadow of Christ in that: 1) He is down in the belly of the prepared fish for three days; 2) He has seaweed around his head much like a crown of thorns; and 3) He has a message of salvation to deliver to the lost people of Nineveh.

In chapter 2 in which Jonah is "running to" God, there are only ten verses and yet, Jonah uses 25 personal pronouns in these 10 verses. "I" is used 10 times, "me" is used 8 times, "my" is used 6 times, and "mine" is used once. I think it can be inferred that the coming revival of Nineveh began with one individual trusting and obeying God. Any of us Christians should never underestimate what may result from our trusting and obeying our Lord's leading.

Jennings (Jay) Turner   2019

WISE MEN WORSHIP HIM
NUGGET 78

The book of Proverbs is filled with examples of wisdom and knowledge and exhortations to seek them. Proverbs 3:19-20 (KJV) reads; "The Lord by wisdom hath founded the earth; by understanding hath he established the heavens. By his knowledge the depths are broken up, and the clouds drop down the dew." Proverbs 9:10 (KJV) reads; "The fear of the Lord is the beginning of wisdom: and the knowledge of the holy is understanding."

Wise men seek to know the will of God. That is wisdom. The greatest gift possible to ever receive is the saving knowledge of Jesus. Wisdom is seeking His will for your life. Surely, if we are wise, the evidence of a saving encounter with the Lord Jesus should manifest itself in our paths and actions.

Jennings (Jay) Turner   2019

KNOW THEM BY THEIR FRUITS
NUGGET 79

Please read Matthew 7:15-20. Verse 16 (KJV) reads;"Ye shall know them by their fruits. Do men gather grapes of thorns, or figs of thistles?"

A corrupt tree cannot bring forth good fruit. A good tree brings forth good fruit. We should pay more attention to a persons actions than to their words. The actual intent of a persons heart will eventually manifest itself in their actions. Mere words are cheap.

Jennings (Jay) Turner   2019

OUR CIRCUMSTANCES ARE UNDER THE FEET OF JESUS
NUGGET 80

Jesus walked on the troubled water as he approached the boat that held the frightened disciples as they were in the midst of a bad storm. I believe that the fact that Jesus was walking on the water is symbolic that all of their circumstances were under his feet. Are not all of our circumstances also under his feet? Jesus has told us where we are going. Therefore, as we sail through this life on our way to our eventual destination, should we not have faith that our earthly circumstances are under the feet of our blessed Jesus? Scripture tells us that if we are saved, we are a part of the body of christ. Since even the water was under his feet, no matter which part of his body that you help make up, circumstances must be under you. If Jesus is your companion on this earthly journey, take heart, hold fast to your faith and put your circumstances into proper perspective.

Jennings (Jay) Turner   2019

BARREN FIG TREE
NUGGET 81

In Luke 21:29-33 we see the parable of the fig tree. We are told to behold the fig tree and when you see it shoot forth you know that summer is at hand. Jesus, being God, knew there were no figs on the distant tree even though it was leafed out. He approaches with the disciples as a lesson for them and us. The tree is expected to have produced fruit. So likewise, we are told, when we see things come to pass, we know the kingdom of God is at hand. The true church, the body of Christ, has filled out like leaves on a tree. This tree is expected to have fruit. How much fruit have we produced? The barren fig tree was cursed by Jesus. Jesus is the vine and we are the branches. Our fruit is found on our branches. There should be fruit on each branch. Does this mean that a seeker must go out on a limb to obtain this eternally satisfying fruit?

Jennings (Jay) Turner   2020

A MIRACULOUS DRAUGHT
NUGGET 82

Following is the first eleven verses of Luke 5 (KJV): 1) And it came to pass, that, as the people pressed upon him (Jesus) to hear the word of God, he stood by the lake of Gennesaret, 2) And saw two ships standing by the lake: but the fishermen were gone out of them, and were washing their nets. 3) And he entered into one of the ships, which was Simon's, and prayed him that he would thrust out a little from the land. And he sat down, and taught the people out of the ship. 4) Now when he had left speaking, he said unto Simon, launch out into the deep, and let down your nets for a draught. 5) And Simon answering said unto him, Master, we have toiled all the night, and have taken nothing: nevertheless at thy word I will let down the net. 6) And when they had this done, they inclosed a great multitude of fishes: and their net brake. 7) And they beckoned unto their partners, which were in the other ship, that they should come and help them. And they came, and filled both the ships, so that they began to sink. 8) When Simon Peter saw it, he fell down at Jesus' knees, saying, Depart from me; for I am a sinful man, O Lord. 9) For he was astonished, and all that were with him, at the draught of the fishes which they had taken: 10) And so was also James, and John, the sons of Zebedee, which were partners with Simon. And Jesus said unto Simon, fear not; from henceforth thou shalt catch men. 11) And when they had brought their ships to land, they forsook all, and followed him.

Next, here are some thoughts concerning the above scripture which you have probably heard or contemplated before: 1) from verse 2 it can be inferred that Jesus picks busy people; 2) Peter allowed Jesus to use his prize possession; 3) in verse 4 Jesus told Peter to let down his "nets", yet Peter only let down one net. Did a lack of sufficient faith cause him to believe that only one would be necessary? Maybe he thought that it would only take one net to show that there were no fish to be caught. Another possible reason is that they had just cleaned their nets.

Nonetheless, Peter did at least put a net down and said, "at thy word"; 4) in verse 6 Peter's net is so filled that it breaks. If he had put down "nets" as he was told, would they have been broken? 5) in verse 7 both ships are filled to the point of sinking. Could this be gratitude from Jesus? Jesus borrowed one ship but filled two. Perhaps this is an example of how God is able to do exceeding, abundantly above all that we ask or think (Ephesians 3:20); 6) in verse 8 Peter is convicted of his sin and bows to Jesus; 7) after Peter has confessed that he is a sinner, in verse 10 Jesus tells him from henceforth Peter will catch men. He is now suitable for service.

Jennings (Jay) Turner   2020

THE EFFECT OF THE SPIRIT
NUGGET 83

In John 3:6 Jesus tells Nicodemus that what is born of the flesh is flesh and what is born of the Spirit is spirit. Then in verse 8 Jesus says; "the wind blows where it will; and though you hear its sound, yet you neither know where it comes from nor where it goes. So it is with every one who is born of the Spirit."

Although we cannot see the wind, we can see its effect on things such as a flag, a tree, or smoke. Therefore, although we cannot see the Spirit of God, we should be able to see its effect on those who have been born of the Spirit. The more that each Christian is influenced by the Holy Spirit, the more obvious it should appear to the rest of the world that our faith is effecting our actions.

Jennings (Jay) Turner   2020

CONCERN FOR THE ABOMINATIONS AROUND US
NUGGET 84

Ezekiel 9:4 reads as follows: (KJV) "And the Lord said unto him, Go through the midst of the city, through the midst of Jerusalem, and set a mark upon the foreheads of the men that sigh and that cry for all the abominations that be done in the midst thereof." The mark was so that these people would be spared and not slain along with all the others. God's instructions inform those that are to do the slaying that they are to begin at his sanctuary.

How appalled are Christians today by the Godless behavior that surrounds us? You can't help but see it in nearly every facet of life. What should we do about it?

First and foremost, we need to share the gospel. 1 Thessalonians 2:4 says that we were put in trust with the gospel. Also, 1Timothy tells us that supplications, prayers, intercessions, and giving of thanks be made for all men. It also informs us that God our Saviour wills all men to be saved and come to the knowledge of the truth.

Therefore, let us all concentrate on inviting, sharing and loving everyone while living and telling the gospel. This appears to me to be a good blueprint for shaping the world around us. Jonah did not want the people of Nineveh to repent. He wanted them to be judged. God changed his mind. What about us? Do we wish to see certain people be judged? If so, God can change your mind. By faith, trust God and put his will before your own. Do you pray, "forgive me my trespasses as I forgive those who trespass against me?" Pretty challenging, huh?

Jennings (Jay) Turner   2020

GOD SAVES THE FAITHFUL
NUGGET 85

In the KJV Ezekiel 14:14 reads: "Though these three men, Noah, Daniel, and Job, were in it, they should deliver but their own souls by their righteousness, saith the Lord God."

Noah overcame the world.

Daniel overcame the flesh.

Job overcame the devil.

Wouldn't you say that God delivers his own? Let's all stand fast and hold firm because God has this.

Jennings (Jay) Turner   2020

HOPE AND WAIT
NUGGET 86

Let's look at a few verses in Psalms concerning hope and waiting upon our Lord. (KJV)

Psalm 42:5 Why art thou cast down, O my soul? and why art thou disquieted in me? hope thou in God: for I shall yet praise him for the help of his countenance.

Psalm 42;11 Why are you cast down O my soul? and why art thou disquieted within me? hope thou in God: for I shall yet praise him, who is the health of my countenance, and my God.

Psalm 43:5 Why art thou cast down, O my soul? and why art thou disquieted within me? hope in God: for I shall yet praise him, who is the health of my countenance, and my God.

Psalm 62:1 Truly my soul waiteth upon God: from him cometh thy salvation.

Psalm 62:5 My soul, wait thou only upon God; for my expectation is from him.

Psalm 62:8 Trust in him at all times; ye people, pour out your heart before him: God is a refuge for us. Selah (think of that!)

In the first verse, the countenance of God helps us and then in the next two, God becomes the health of our countenance. Obviously, the psalmist is cast down but his hope in God becomes a source of health. Next, David is waiting upon God. His expectation is from God. In verse 62:8 David expresses his trust in God and he encourages all to pour out their hearts while waiting. Let God know your burdens. He is a refuge for us. These verses can be a great help to us as we go through difficult times.

Jennings (Jay) Turner   2020

PRAY AND WAIT
NUGGET 87

⸻ ❧ ⸻

The Bible has many places where God's people are depressed, afraid, and desperate. This happens over and over to individuals as well as to peoples and nations. When God is approached with an attitude of repentance and faith, the seekers can find peace while they ponder on his past miracles and wait upon his help. The following is just a couple of examples taken from Psalms 62 and 77.

In Psalm 77, Asaph, the writer, is depressed. He begins in verse one crying out to God. Next he seeks God. In verses three thru five, he complains as he remembers the days of old and is overwhelmed by the trial he is facing. Verse seven has him wondering if the Lord has cast off forever and is angry and therefore has removed his tender mercies. Beginning in verse eleven; 11) "I will remember the works of the Lord; Surely I will remember your wonders of old. 12) I will also meditate on all your work, And talk of your deeds. 13) Your way, O God, is in the sanctuary; Who is so great a God as our God? 14) You are the God who does wonders; you have declared your strength among the peoples. 15) You have with your arm redeemed your people, The sons of Jacob and Joseph. Selah. 16) The waters saw you, O God; The waters saw you, they were afraid; The depths also trembled. 17) The clouds poured out water; The skies sent out a sound; your arrows also flashed about. 18) The voice of your thunder was in the whirlwind; The lightnings lit up the world; The earth trembled and shook. 19) Your way was in the sea, your path in the great waters, And your footsteps were not known. 20) You led Your people like a flock By the hand of Moses and Aaron." Try to see the progression of Asaph in the Psalm. Next, we will look at Psalm 62 for another step.

As you read the twelve verses of Psalm 62 (a Psalm of David) pay particular attention to verses 1, 5, and 7 which read; 1) "Truly my soul silently waits for God; From him comes my salvation; 5) My soul, wait silently for God alone, For my expectation is from him; 7) In God is my salvation and my glory; The rock of my strength, And my refuge, is in God."

These scriptures speak to me about some things to remember when I find myself in what seems to be a dire circumstance. I can cry out to God, seek him, and pour out my concerns and complaints to him. Next, I can wait upon him and while waiting, be encouraged by remembering his past mercies, miracles, and acts of love. Always hold fast and stand firm.

The body of Christ should not just sit back with the attitude; "it must be the end times". We should be leading the way with prayers and supplications to God. 2 Chronicles 7:14 tells us (God's people) how to act. It says we are to humble ourselves, pray, seek God's face, turn from our wicked ways and then he will forgive us and heal our land. People in crisis are usually seeking. We need to be ready to share God's answer for peace which is to gain a relationship with him through his son Jesus Christ.

Jennings (Jay) Turner   2020

THE WOMAN AT THE WELL
NUGGET 88

⁘ ❈ ⁘

This story of the "woman at the well" is told in John 4:10-39. Many different applications have been learned from this story. I would like to share one.

Jesus, alone, encounters a Samaritan woman at a well. In the environment of that time, Jews and Samaritans did not mix. In verse 9 she addresses Jesus as a *"Jew". Something begins to stir within her as she experiences Jesus. In verse 11 she calls him "Sir". Jesus tells her that he can offer her living water and she wishes to receive it. Jesus, in a kindly way, tells her that she has had five husbands and is currently living with a sixth. She is probably under conviction. In verse 19 she acknowledges Jesus to be a "Prophet". By verse 29 she has gone into the city to tell others that Jesus is the Christ.*

This woman has been saved and she goes into the city to tell the people about Jesus. Note that she dropped even her pot in her urgency to tell everyone. I think that there is little doubt that this woman was looked down upon by the townspeople and was probably somewhat of an outcast. Now with the Holy Spirit in her, consider the love and forgiveness she exhibits as she brings the good news of Jesus the Christ to the people who had probably refused to associate with her.

This is an inspiration to me because I too am a sinner saved by grace and I, like this woman, with help and guidance from the Holy Spirit, wish to forgive others and share the gospel without judgement or prejudice. It has been two thousand years since that encounter at the well but that woman is our sister in Christ! Won't it be great to meet her in heaven?

Jennings (Jay) Turner   2020

STAY IN FELLOWSHIP
NUGGET 89

In John chapter 21 Jesus has risen and Peter has left the ministry of catching men and returned to trying to catch fish. Thomas, Nathaniel, the sons of Zebedee and two other disciples are with him. Peter tells them that he is going fishing. The others decide to go out with him. It is noteworthy that Peter has pulled others along with him away from fishing for men. They fish all night and catch nothing. When they return in the morning, the resurrected Jesus is standing on the shore but they do not recognize him. Note also here the disciples, under human leadership, did not prosper. Jesus asked them if they had any food. They responded "No". Jesus then told them, "Cast the net on the right side of the boat and you will find some." They obeyed and the net contained 153 large fish. They then knew it was the Lord Jesus and they rushed to Him. When they obeyed and followed Jesus, they prospered.

You might also note that the net did not break. Christ is sufficient for any and all who come to Him. Why did Jesus instruct them to cast the net over the right side of the boat? Could it be a reference to "the right hand of fellowship". I do not know but it could have to do with following the precise leading of Jesus without adding or taking away any detail.

Jennings (Jay) Turner   2020

NEWLY REVEALED TRUTH
NUGGET 90

Anyone who regularly reads and studies scripture has read the same portions of the Bible over and over. The Word of God is a living thing. Many times it is referred to as "seed". We may not "read" anything new, but something new may be "revealed" to us. This new insight should help us to see ourselves, our circumstances, and others from God's perspective. Then, with the help of the Holy Spirit, this new light should be reflected in our thoughts and actions. These new "nuggets" are worth more than gold and silver. They contribute to our spiritual growth, increase our faith, and promote our peace with our loving God. Wow, what an adventure and joy!

Jennings (Jay) Turner   2020

ONE GOD
NUGGET 91

There are many things in life that are okay to enjoy or attain so long as we do not allow them to become such a focus that they become a god to us. We can all make a list of some of these potential hazards. Especially the ones we can identify in others. Things such as wealth, power, prestige, fame, and on and on.

Isaiah 44:8-10 (NKJV) reads; "Do not fear, nor be afraid; Have I not told you from that time, and declared it? You are My witnesses. Is there a God besides Me? Indeed there is no other Rock; I know not one. Those who make an image, all of them are useless, And their precious things shall not profit; They are their own witnesses; They neither see nor know, that they may be ashamed. Who would form a god or mold an image that profits him nothing?"

Now look at Psalms 115:3-8 (NKJV); "But our God is in heaven; He does whatever He pleases. Their idols are silver and gold, The work of men's hands. They have mouths, but they do not speak; Eyes they have, but they do not see; They have ears, but they do not hear; Noses they have, but they do not smell; They have hands, but they do not handle; Feet they have, but they do not walk; Nor do they mutter through their throat. Those who make them are like them; So is everyone who trusts in them."

It says above: "those who make them are like them." I believe that this means that if anyone puts something before God, that person, when it comes to things of God such as instruction, correction or the gospel, will not hear, see, nor understand. When a time of critical need comes along, how would any of these other gods be able to help, console or save? Never allow anything to come before the God of our creation.

Jennings (Jay) Turner   2020

MADE FIT BY JESUS
NUGGET 92

We do not become right or fit before God because of any works or deeds we do. God has provided a way for us to be fit in His eyes and His way only involves us believing and trusting in and on His provision. That provision is His sinless son Jesus who was a willing sacrifice, shedding His blood for the sins of anyone who, by faith, receives this free gift. Jesus Christ was raised from the dead and sits at the right hand of God. Believe and trust in this provision and you too will now and for eternity be fit and fellowship with God.

References:
Romans 3:23
Romans 6:23
Romans 10:9
John 3:16
Ephesians 2:8-9

This is the greatest gift ever given. Receive it and then share it.

Jennings (Jay) Turner   2020

OLD DO-IT-YOURSELF MENTALITY GONE
NUGGET 93

Our testimony ought not be only the circumstance of what led us to Christ and the relief we received, but also the fact that God, through the Spirit of Christ, lives within you giving you great peace in spite of continuing problems and sin. You are delivered from that old dead life. The old do-it-yourself mentality of worry is somehow relieved and your viewpoint, when seen from God's perspective, becomes long term (eternal) and the bumps and trials of this life are put into a different light.

God was with Moses, then Joshua, and on and on with those who would trust and obey. God didn't seem to grant some utopia of circumstances but rather used the often troubled surrounding circumstances to "work out their growth and salvation". If we believe that God is also with us, shouldn't we also have courage?

Read Romans 8:8-17

Jennings (Jay) Turner   2020

FAITH IN ACTION
NUGGET 94

———— ❦ ————

Romans 10:17 reads "So then faith cometh by hearing and hearing by the word of God." My faith is based on the Word of God. That is one of the reasons that I must look continually into the Word of God. This will grow my faith. Please read Ephesians 6:11-17. It is in these passages that we are told to put on the armor of God. Verse 16 says; "above all, taking the shield of faith with which you will be able to quench all the fiery darts of the wicked one." For this faith (shield) to be effective, you must raise it up and use it.

The following is what I believe each of us should do: Watch for something that you feel the Holy Spirit is leading you do but for which you feel inadequate. This will require us to rely on God. It will require some faith to step out in a way in which we feel inadequate on our own. God will be pleased in this exercise of faith and He will not fail us. Thus, in turn, our faith will grow.

Jennings (Jay) Turner   2020

DON'T MOLD GOD'S WORD TO FIT OUR LIFESTYLE
NUGGET 95

I believe that most people, internally, desire to adhere to the will of God. I also know that there are pressures and influences that hinder that desire. We could all name several. Two of these are peer pressure and tradition.

A powerful aspect of peer pressure is the desire to be seen in a positive light by those around us. We all wish to be accepted socially. To this end we may be willing to compromise beliefs in order to retain our perceived social position. Please read Mark 6:14-28. Here we read the story of King Herod's troubled conscience concerning the beheading of John the Baptist. Verse 26 (NIV) reads; "The king was greatly distressed, but because of his oath and his dinner guests, he did not want to refuse her." The king did not wish to behead John the Baptist but other pressures were compelling him.

When speaking to the Pharisees and Scribes in Mark 7:8-9 (NIV) Jesus says; "You have let go of the commands of God and are holding on to the traditions of men." And he said to them (9): "You have a fine way of setting aside the commands of God in order to observe your own traditions!"

A lesson in this is that we should never try to mold the commands of God so that they fit either the way in which we wish to go or to conform to behavior that we feel others expect of us. The flesh is truly weak but our desire and efforts should always be to abide in the will of God.

Jennings (Jay) Turner   2020

TELL EVERYONE OR NO ONE?
NUGGET 96

Mark 7:36 (KJV) reads: "And he charged them that they should tell no man: but the more he charged them, so much the more a great deal they published it." Next, please look at Matthew 28:18-20 (KJV) that states the following: "And Jesus came and spake unto them, saying, All power is given unto me in heaven and in earth. Go ye therefore, and teach all nations, baptizing them in the name of the Father, and of the Son, and of the Holy Ghost: Teaching them to observe all things whatsoever I have commanded you: and lo, I am with you alway, even unto the end of the world."

During his earthly ministry, Jesus healed, blessed and changed the lives of many. He often instructed them that they should tell no one but instead, they told many. In Matthew 28 Jesus charges the disciples to go unto all the world and tell the good news of his teaching. The irony of this is convicting to me. We all need to "go and tell." Each of us should trust that God will help us to share and step out. If we have an eternal perspective, I don't see how we could ever regret it.

Jennings (Jay) Turner   2020

FEAR NOT
NUGGET 97

Luke 1:30 (KJV) reads: "And the angel said unto her, Fear not Mary: for thou hast found favor with God." If we have found favor with God, we should "fear not". If anyone has faith that Jesus Christ is the risen Son of God, thereby creating an attitude of repentance and calls upon him for salvation, he or she will become a new creation (born again) and the Holy Spirit of God will indwell them.

If you have received salvation, the Holy Spirit dwells within you and you will know it. He will be a comfort and will open your eyes to understand many things and attitudes. You will recognize a change within yourself. You have become a member of the true church: that is, the body of Christ. As a member of the body of Christ you have certainly gained the favor the Father. Therefore, as we grow and learn more and more to trust in Him, our fears of this world should lessen. We should try and see circumstances from an eternal perspective. We know from the ending of the Book of Revelation the glorious future awaiting those found in the Lamb's Book of Life. Don't delay seeking God through Jesus Christ. Jesus shed His innocent blood in order to provide a worthy sacrifice for our sins thereby providing a way for us to be reconciled to a Holy Father. No matter what your past or present sins may be, the blood of Jesus is able to cover them. You can do nothing to earn it. It is a free gift. Just believe and receive it.

Jennings (Jay) Turner   2020

WHAT WOULD WE DO TO SAVE A FRIEND?
NUGGET 98

The following is Luke 5:18-20 (KJV): "And, behold, men brought in a bed a man which was taken with a palsy: and they sought means to bring him in, and to lay him before him (Jesus). And when they could not find by what way they might bring him in because of the multitude, they went upon the housetop, and let him down through the tiling with his couch into the midst before Jesus. And when he saw their faith, he said unto him, Man, thy sins are forgiven thee."

This story convicts me concerning what I am willing to do to bring a friend or family member to Jesus. I have personally witnessed to many people but there have been times when I have been hesitant and missed opportunities. Why was I hesitant? Was I afraid of being rejected or being thought of as "odd" or "over the top"? I don't really know but I do know that I am not ashamed of the gospel. I pray that the scripture above will bring whatever is necessary for each of us to walk closer with our savior.

Jennings (Jay) Turner   2020

DON'T BE SWALLOWED BY A GREAT FISH
NUGGET 99

When I see all of the senseless rioting, burning, looting, and killing going on in our nation, it makes me yearn for the Kingdom of God to come quickly. I desire for truth to be made known to everyone and for justice to prevail for all. However, Christians must try and see all aspects of our surroundings from God's perspective.

I don't believe that any of us think that we consistently see life from God's perspective. That is why we continue to search His word and desire Him to reveal wisdom and truths to us. I, in my flesh, wish to see these perpetrators brought to justice, However, God's word gives me pause in some regards.

First, I don't wish to receive justice for me. I, instead, pray for mercy. This makes me wonder why I am willing to have justice applied to others. 1 Timothy chapter 2 exhorts us to make supplications, prayers, intercessions, and give thanks for all men.

Secondly, I am reminded of the book of Jonah. God instructed Jonah to go and cry against the city of Nineveh. The sin of the city was very great. Jonah knew this and did not wish to see them repent. He wanted their sins to be judged. Therefore, Jonah ran in the opposite direction. He did not wish to see them repent and be spared. God helped Jonah to see the situation from His perspective and then Jonah obeyed.

I don't have any qualms about seeing those who break the law being penalized for their actions. However, I believe that the body of the church needs to make supplications that all will know the gospel and repent and I think that all those involved in terrible acts need us, the body of Christ, to care and share. Let's go out and BE the Church.

Jennings (Jay) Turner   2020

CONFESS AND REST
NUGGET 100

Please read the first 5 verses of Psalm 32. We learn herein that blessed are those whose transgression is forgiven, whose sin is covered.

David, the author of this psalm, then tells of how, because he kept silent, his bones waxed old through his groaning all the day long. He says that the hand of God's displeasure was heavy upon him day and night. In verse 5, David uses 8 personal pronouns. He thereby acknowledges that he is solely to blame for his iniquities and transgressions. He openly confesses this to the Lord. Because he has confessed unto the Lord, the Lord forgave him the iniquity of his sin.

By confessing our sin and finding forgiveness, each and every one of us can find peace that passes all understanding. Confessing and turning toward God will not end troubles in this life. However, receiving the Holy Spirit into your heart and life will give you access to peace, regardless of your surrounding circumstances, that you have not before known. This is the testimony of countless Christians. Seeing life and eternity from the perspective of God is the greatest balm that exists. Jesus came into the world not to condemn us. He came in order to die as a sacrifice for us. His blood is sufficient for ALL our sins. We need only to freely receive this gift of God through faith. God desires to save you right now no matter the depth of your sin. He saves sinners. Don't even think about doing some "cleanup" before you seek Him. Do you think that you can clean yourself from sin by the will of your flesh? You cannot be too sinful to come to Him. God wishes to do the cleaning through His Son Jesus. Come now! All of heaven rejoices when who was lost is found.

Jennings (Jay) Turner   2020

MAKE US READY FOR ETERNITY
NUGGET 101

Over the years I have always been hesitant to pray for patience. I would think that most of us desire patience but are somewhat wary of the circumstances that may be necessary to attain it. I have heard many people say that they are afraid to pray for patience for fear of the lesson that may follow. The same may be said of character. My grandfather was a coal miner who died from black lung disease in 1929. He left behind seven children and the great depression was just beginning. That family pulled together and helped each other in every way. They all became successful, productive, people full of love and character. Now, I'm sure that their strong character evolved to a large degree owing to the dire circumstances they encountered and overcame. Now, although my spirit aspires to possess patience and character, my flesh isn't so willing.

Personally, I can relate this thinking to my relationship with God. I believe it boils down to this dilemma: I desire to become the most usable tool possible so that He may use me in some way for His glory but in my flesh I am hesitant to yield control to Him because I don't wish to give up control of where things may lead. Intellectually this makes no sense. I know that God loves me more than I can possibly imagine. I also know that his will for my life and future is the very best course for me. Yet, my flesh does not relish the idea of me not being the one sitting on the throne of my life.

Are you now or have you ever found yourself at these crossroads? There is no doubt, from an eternal perspective, that the wisest decision is to go "all in". Jesus told us that when we are a guest we should not choose to take a seat of honor but rather wait to be invited to do so. Do we wish to have our Savior sit at the head of our table? Then let each of us invite Him to occupy the throne of our will.

God's Word tells us that without faith, it is impossible to please Him. Therefore, let us all, by faith, yield to Him and pray for Him to prepare us for eternity.

Jennings (Jay) Turner   2020

DON'T CHOOSE WHICH SOIL TO SOW UPON
NUGGET 102

In Matthew 13-3-9 we find the familiar parable of the sower and the soils. We know that the seed is the word of the Kingdom because we are told so in verse 19. The seed is the gospel (good news). The seed is incorruptible (1 Pet 1:23); it is the gospel that brings forth fruit in souls (Col 1:5-6). The sower is our Lord Jesus Christ, either by himself, or by the Church (His body of believers).

Four types of soil are mentioned in the story: wayside, stony places, thorny ground, and good ground. Please notice that the sower did not sow the seed only on the good ground. Because the seed fell on all ground, I believe that as Christians, whenever we have an opportunity to sow the gospel seed, we should never judge what type of soil we believe our opportunity has presented us with. If we are obedient, we must, with love, sow on any ground upon which we have opportunity.

You are not a salesman. You do not need to "know it all". The gospel is the power of God unto salvation. It is creative. Just sow with love.

Jennings (Jay) Turner   2020

CREATION GLORY
NUGGET 103

A portion of Romans 1:20 reads: "For ever since the world was created, people have seen the earth and sky. Through everything God made, they can clearly see his invisible qualities – his eternal power and divine nature."

I have always loved to be outside enjoying nature. Especially trees. In fact, I once planted more than 6,000 trees on some land I once owned. I am writing this in the middle of October and the color has been magnificent. This nugget is merely to suggest to you that the trees have up stretched their arms in praise of God.

Jennings (Jay) Turner   2020

ORDER OF PRAYER
NUGGET 104

—❈—

Matthew 6:9-13 contain what is familiarly known as The Lord's Prayer. Jesus tells us in verse 9; "in this manner, therefore, pray". I am sure that there are various insights as to what Jesus meant by "in this manner". In this nugget I attempt to share one such insight.

First, let's consider the ordering of the Ten Commandments. They begin by telling us we cannot have any gods before our Father God. Next, we are not to bow down to or serve any images. Thirdly, we are commanded to not take the name of the Lord your God in vain. The order of the commandments begins with the recognition of the holiness of God and our required response to Him.

Next, let's look at the structure of the prayer Jesus taught in Matthew chapter 6. The ordering is similar. In the very beginning we are to acknowledge God as our Father in heaven and ask that His name be hallowed. Secondly, we ask that God's kingdom and His will come to us and be manifested here on earth. After this beginning, we ask that His divine mercy will help with our forgiveness, spiritual growth and deliverance.

Most Christians have memorized this beautiful prayer. Maybe the "manner" of which Jesus refers suggests that we possess the attitude of always placing God and His will first in everything. Recognizing and desiring the proper ordering can be a blueprint of how to worship and honor God and invite Him to sit upon the throne of our hearts. Be careful to not recite scripture by rote and thereby not catch all that the Holy Spirit wishes to show you.

Jennings (Jay) Turner   2020

TRUTH WILL PREVAIL
NUGGET 105

I pray that this nugget may bring encouragement concerning the future and what, as Christians, our current focus should be. As Christians, we are not *of* this world but we are *in* this world. When we see unfairness, false accusations, cheating, cruelness, etc, we can and should try to right it; but as Christians, we should also keep our main focus on sharing the gospel and loving others, even our enemies. We should lift *everyone* up with prayer and love that they may hear and believe the gospel message. After all, we may gain a brother or sister and lose an enemy. Besides, we are instructed of God that this His will.

I have to confess that when I see injustice I am frustrated when I don't see an immediate consequence and correction *on my timeline*, not God's. We know from scripture that God warns of the consequences of deceit and lies. Proverbs 11:1 says,"Dishonest scales are an abomination to the Lord". Proverbs 11:27 says, "Trouble will come to him who seeks evil". Proverbs 19:5 says, "A false witness will not go unpunished and he who speaks lies will not escape".

Let's look at Psalms 35 where we find David pleading with God to help him against those (Saul) who are unjustly trying to take his life. Verses 7 and 8 read, "For without cause they have hidden their net for me in a pit, which they have dug without cause for my life. Let destruction come upon him unexpectedly, and let his net that he has hidden catch himself; into that very destruction let him fall." We know that Saul did lay a net for David. His plot was to have David fall at the hands of the Philistines (1 Samuel 18:25). This net he laid was under the pretense of doing David honor. True to God's word, it was Saul who fell at the hands of the Philistines. Notice that David himself never raised his hand against Saul. David found joy in his soul, not because he was safe, but in the Lord and his salvation.

We can have joy knowing, through faith, that God is at work and always keeps His promises. Our main concern here in this worldly kingdom is to love others. Even our enemies. And to share the gospel at every opportunity. As the world gets darker, the light within Christians should only shine brighter. I can certainly seek truth and justice but my primary focus should be loving others and sharing our beautiful gospel message.

Jennings (Jay) Turner   2020

HOLD FAST AND STAND FIRM
NUGGET 106

The following verses have been quoted from Eugene Peterson's <u>The</u> <u>Message.</u> Hebrews 6:13-15 "When God made his promise to Abraham, he backed it to the hilt, putting his own reputation on the line. He said, 'I promise that I'll bless you with everything I have — bless and bless and bless!' Abraham stuck it out and got everything that had been promised to him." Next, let us look at Hebrews 11: 8-10 that reads: "By an act of faith, Abraham said yes to God's call to travel to an unknown place that would become his home. When he left he had no idea where he was going. By an act of faith he lived in the country promised him, lived as a stranger camping in tents. Isaac and Jacob did the same, living under the same promise. Abraham did it by keeping his eye on an unseen city with real, eternal foundations — the City designed and built by God."

Abraham, through faith, was justified. He endured many trials but was patient. Why would we, living in the twenty-first century expect anything different? Christians are "in" this world but are not "of" this world. Our lives here on earth are like a vapor that is seen for only a moment. Anyone who has received Jesus Christ should consider the circumstances they encounter on earth from an eternal viewpoint. Jesus, although sinless, suffered and died for our sins. So then, why would a Christian not expect to encounter some suffering here? Hold fast to your faith, be patient, and focus on laying up treasures in heaven. Love all people and share the gospel. Be faithful and patient. Help and encourage one another, whenever and however possible. Our redemption draws near.

Tears may sometimes be the beginning of a rainbow in your soul.

Jennings (Jay) Turner   2021

PART OF BEARING YOUR CROSS
NUGGET 107

"Jesus, for the joy set before him, endured the cross, despising the shame, and is set down at the right hand of the throne of God."(Hebrews 12:2 KJV).

Christians, for the joy set before them, must also be prepared to endure their current circumstances as well as whatever may yet come. This is part of bearing your cross.

Jesus endured the cross for all who would believe and trust on him. Jesus, our Master and Savior, has asked that we follow his teaching and love others as ourselves. This isn't always easy. Yielding to the will of God necessitates that we die to the desires of the flesh. Luke 17:33 KJV says; "whosoever shall seek to save his life shall lose it; and whosoever shall lose his life shall preserve it." Our salvation was purchased with the greatest price ever paid. Don't be conformed to this world. Loving the Lord with everything you have and your very life is your reasonable service (Romans 12:1).

"What you lack in understanding can be compensated for in obedience." Charles Swindoll

Jennings (Jay) Turner   2021

OUR CORNER STONE
NUGGET 108

The rock in the wilderness was struck so that water would flow from it and save God's wandering people. Jesus Christ is the corner stone and He was struck so that the Spirit of life would flow from Him to all who drink.

Ephesians 2:20 (KJV) tells us that Jesus Christ himself is the chief corner stone. The hymn "Rock of Ages" reflects this truth. In the hymn, the rock obviously refers to Jesus Christ. The "rock" has been cleft. I view the cleft as the ultimate place of peace and safety in which to abide. The hymn tells us "could my zeal no languor know, could my tears forever flow, these for sins could not atone, thou must save and thou alone." Another stanza says; "in my hand no price I bring, simply to thy cross I cling." Ephesians 2:8-9 (KJV) reads as follows; "For by grace are ye saved through faith; and that not of yourselves: it is the gift of God: Not of works, lest any man should boast."

Jennings (Jay) Turner   2021

SINS, PROBLEMS AND GRACE
NUGGET 109

Whatever problems you are facing, remember that Jesus died on the cross so that His blood could be the atonement for your sins. God gave us this unfathomable gift by grace so that we may receive salvation freely without works. That is a love so profound that I can only marvel at it and praise Him for His great mercy.

So, no matter what problems or situations you may be facing, God can and wishes to help you with them. Yield to Christ and see yourself, others, and the world from God's perspective. The Holy Spirit will reside in you and open your eyes and heart and help you to overcome or abide in all circumstances. If you are already a believer, make yourself available as a tool to God so that He can use you. You are just a tool. By faith, make yourself willing to be used. God has this. If you have never made a decision to ask Jesus into your life, do it now. Tomorrow is never guaranteed. The decision for Christ carries with it a long-term consequence that is better than you can ever imagine. Even any short-term difficulty you may face in this short life, when seen from God's perspective, cannot disturb the joy and peace that comes from fellowship with Him. His Holy Spirit will reside in you and give you the most joyful life possible.

Jennings (Jay) Turner   2021

REAP WHAT YOU SOW
NUGGET 110

When Isaac was old, and his eyes were dim, he called Esau, his eldest son, and asked him to go hunting for venison. Isaac directed, "Prepare me the kind of tasty food I like and bring it to me to eat, so that I may give you my blessing before I die." (NIV)

Rebekah, Isaac's wife, overheard Isaac's plan. Therefore, she concocted a plan to deceive Isaac into giving the blessing to Jacob instead of Esau. They put upon Jacob some of Esau's clothing so that Jacob might smell like Esau. They also put some skins of goats on the backs of Jacob's hands and upon his neck so that he would feel hairy like his brother. Jacob then lied to his father concerning his identity and received the blessing intended for Esau.

Later, Laban, his mother's brother, deceived Jacob when he gave Jacob Leah to marry instead of Rachel who had been promised him for his seven years of labor. Laban also used deceit to gain materially from Jacob's sheep and goats.

Galatians 6:7 (KJV) reads, "Be not deceived; God is not mocked: for whatsoever a man soweth, that shall he also reap." Jacob both used and received deception. Consider how amazing the crop would be if we would sow the seeds of love, truth and loyalty.

Jennings (Jay) Turner   2021

GOD IS PATIENT
NUGGET 111

I have been a Christian for many years. When I reflect back on my life, I am amazed at the patience and love that God has shown me. God is love. He loved me when I was far from him.

It slowly became clear to me that God expected me to be patient and loving to others as he had been to me. He means "all others," not just those who look like me, think like me, or are easy to love. God was patient with and loved every saved person before their salvation. Therefore, shouldn't every saved person be patient with and love everyone regardless of their current status or state?

Jennings (Jay) Turner   2021

GOD IN PURSUIT
NUGGET 112

Luke 15:4 (KJV) says, "What man of you, having an hundred sheep, if he lose one of them, doth not leave the ninety and nine in the wilderness, and go after that which is lost, until he find it?" God pursues the lost. 1 Timothy 2:1-4 (KJV) says, "I exhort therefore, that, first of all, supplications, prayers, intercessions, and giving of thanks, be made for all men; For kings, and for all that are in authority; that we may lead a quiet and peaceable life in all godliness and honesty. For this is good and acceptable in the sight of God our Saviour; Who will have all men to be saved, and to come unto the knowledge of the truth."

When we stray, we are more vulnerable to the world and its ways. However, God will not stop pursuing the wayward or lost. Therefore, it is obvious that all who are saved must also pursue the lost and anyone in the body of Christ who has strayed.

Jennings (Jay) Turner   2021

SPIRIT OF LIFE
NUGGET 113

Psalms 78:15-17 (NLT) says, "He split open the rocks in the wilderness to give them water, as from a gushing spring. He made streams pour from the rock, making the waters flow down like a river! Yet they kept on sinning against him, rebelling against the Most High in the desert."

The rock in the wilderness was struck so that water would flow to save them from thirst. 1 Peter 2:7 tells us that Christ is the stone that the builders rejected and became the cornerstone of the Church. Christ, the cornerstone, was struck when he paid the penalty for our sins so that the Spirit of Life may flow from him to all who will drink. Will you Drink?

Jennings (Jay) Turner   2021

LOOKING FOR PEACE IN ALL THE WRONG PLACES
NUGGET 114

Most people in the world around us are in search of things or situations that will give them joy and inner peace. However, even those who have become extremely successful in the world often relate that something is missing. If God is not in your heart, there is a void that longs to be filled. Being successful in secular life is not necessarily a bad thing. Wealth, position or other worldly accomplishments are not a problem unless you put them before God. If your self-confidence is bolstered by any achievement to the point where you move God down on your list of priorities, you have a problem.

Compared with eternity, we are only on this earth for a moment. 1 John 2:15-16 (KJV) says, "Love not the world, neither the things that are in the world. If any man love the world, the love of the Father is not in him. For all that is in the world, the lust of the flesh, and the lust of the eyes, and the pride of life, is not of the Father but is of the world." 1John 5:5 (KJV) says, "Who is he that overcometh the world, but he that believeth that Jesus is the Son of God?"

God wants you to invite him to sit upon the throne of your heart. Who or what is now sitting on your throne?

Also see: Mark 8:36-37; John 12:25; John 15:19; John 16:33;

1 Cor 7:31; Phil 3:8; and James 4:4

Jennings (Jay) Turner   2021

THE SON HAS RISEN
NUGGET 115

The sun rises every day to provide earthly life. The **son** of God, our Lord Jesus Christ, rose once to give us eternal life. He came into the world to be the sacrifice for the sins of man. He was faithful to that end. He was a willing sacrifice. He rose on the third day. Repent, believe in your heart that God has raised Jesus from the dead and his blood will cover all of your sins.

Believe and receive. Lift up your hands and praise Him. In creation, even the trees lift their hands up to God.

Jennings (Jay) Turner   2021

OBSTACLES OR OPPORTUNITIES
NUGGET 116

In the thirteenth chapter of Numbers is the story of the twelve men being sent to spy out the land of Canaan. Their report was that the land was spectacular. The spies also returned with some fruit that was amazing as well. Ten of the spies reported that because of the "giants" living there, the Israelites would not be able to take possession. Of the spies, only Joshua and Caleb had sufficient faith that, with God's help, the victory would be assured.

Using hindsight, I have wondered why the people didn't chose to proceed. After all, they had recently been delivered from the bondage of Egypt through the mighty power of God. Then, feeling shame, I am reminded of times when I have been frightened or stopped by "giants" even when I believed I was being prompted by the Holy Spirit. This is very humbling because I also know that with God, nothing is impossible.

Each Christian must decide if, when God prompts or commands us to serve, God is sufficient. In fact, he is best able to use us when we are weak. Don't you think that God knows beforehand what trials lie ahead? If God calls you to any endeavor, you can be sure that, with his help, you are right for the job.

By the way, the ten who "played it safe" all died in the wilderness. Can you name even one of them?

Jennings (Jay) Turner   2021

JESUS CAN MAGNIFY A LITTLE
NUGGET 117

Romans 12:4-5 says, "For as we have many members in one body, and all members have not the same office: so we, being many, are one body in Christ, and every one members one of another." The spiritual church is made up of the body of believers. Every saved person is a part of the body of Christ. Each member or *cell* of the body has been given a measure of faith and has the Holy Spirit living within him. All around us we can see opportunities to serve. Sometimes, what may stop us from stepping out to serve is a feeling of inadequacy. Guess what? You probably *are* inadequate. God wants to use you. Do you think that Moses was adequate to lead God's people out of Egypt on his own?

Jesus fed the 5,000 with just a little. Just think of how much God can accomplish with the little *you* have if you will only make it available and yielded to him.

Jennings (Jay) Turner   2021

TAKE POSSESSION OF PROMISES
NUGGET 118

Joshua 18:3 says, "And Joshua said unto the children of Israel, How long are ye slack to go to possess the land, which the Lord God of your fathers hath given you?" God's people had been promised ownership of the promised land but had not taken possession of it. Joshua and Caleb wanted to take possession but were over ruled by those whose lack of faith did not allow them to see past "giants" standing in the way.

Hebrews 11:6 says, "But without faith it is impossible to please him: for he that cometh to God must believe that he is, and that he is a rewarder of them that diligently seek him." Most or all of us we have felt urgings from the Holy Spirit that we didn't follow through on because of some perceived or real "giant". In Hebrews 13:5 we are promised that he will never leave nor forsake us. Through prayer, we can ask the Holy Spirit to embolden us to put our faith into action.

When David faced Goliath, nearly all the bystanders were probably thinking, "He is a giant and cannot be beaten." David was probably thinking, "He is so big, how can I miss?" (Nicky Gumbel)

Jennings (Jay) Turner   2021

JESUS BRINGS COMPLETE VICTORY
NUGGET 119

In Greek, the name Joshua means, "The Lord saves." Joshua 13:1 says, "Now Joshua was old and stricken in years; and the Lord said unto him, Thou are old and stricken in years, and there remaineth yet very much land to be possessed." Joshua's victories were not complete. Jesus alone brings complete victory. The Church, the body of Christ, must keep busy doing the will of God until Jesus returns and completes God's plan. The field is ripe. There are more souls to save. Go out and be the Church.

Jennings (Jay) Turner   2021

OURSELVES AND BARABBAS
NUGGET 120

John 18:40 tells us that Barabbas was a notable criminal who had been sentenced to be put to death by crucifixion. Jesus was brought before Pilate and found to be innocent. Nevertheless, the crowd wanted Jesus to be crucified. Tradition dictated that Pilate release one prisoner. The crowd chose to have Barabbus released and to have Jesus crucified.

Romans 3:23 says that all of us have sinned and come short of the glory of God. We were worthy of death. We were just like Barabbus. Also, just like Barabbus, we were freed at the expense of Jesus. This is the greatest gift from God. Jesus died for the sins of each of us. It is a gift that cannot be earned. It is a free gift by God's grace. What will you do with this great gift? Will you receive it by faith with joy and thankfulness?

Jennings (Jay) Turner   2021

HOW SAUL WAS PERSECUTING JESUS
NUGGET 121

Acts 9:1-5 (KJV) says, "And Saul, yet breathing out threatenings and slaughter against the disciples of the Lord, went unto the high priest, and desired of him letters to Damascus to the synagogues, that if he found any of this way, whether they were men or women, he might bring them bound unto Jerusalem. And as he journeyed, he came near Damascus: and suddenly there shined round about him a light from heaven: and he fell to the earth, and heard a voice saying unto him, Saul, Saul, why persecutest thou me? And he said, Who are thou, Lord? And the Lord said, I am Jesus whom thou persecutest: it is hard for thee to kick against the pricks."

Saul had not yet met Jesus. Therefore, how could he be persecuting him? The answer is that he was persecuting the Church, of which Jesus is the head, while the body is made up of believers.

Saul was blinded for three days and then received both his sight and the Holy Ghost. You too can become a part of the body of Christ. You need only to call upon the name of Jesus, place your trust in Him, and believe that God raised Him from the dead, and not only will you receive eternal life, but you will know the joy, peace and fullness of life that come from being part of God's kingdom.

Jennings (Jay) Turner   2021

HAVE YOU BEEN BLESSED?
NUGGET 122

Have you been blessed? If so, you need to be a blessing to others. Everyone who has received the holy spirit has a spiritual gift. We each need to exercise this gift. Each individual making up the body of Christ (the Church) has a gift, which, when used in concert with the rest of the body, allows the Church to function effectively. Are you only a consumer or are you also a contributor?

Jennings (Jay) Turner

LIFE SHOULDN'T BE A GAME
NUGGET 123

We have all played board games for fun. The winning strategy in many of these games is to accumulate more things than your opponents. Sometimes these accumulations are tangible. For instance, money, houses, hotels and property (Monopoly.) Other times, it involves intangible goals such as education, high paying jobs, prestige, fame, and power (game of Life.)

What we must remember is that when any of these games is over, everything goes back into the box. Nothing can be carried forward. This is the reality of life. We came into this world naked and it is naked that we will leave it. Trying to achieve these things is not a problem as long as none of them becomes a god to you. Whatever we acquire in this world from striving in the flesh is meaningless in eternity. Matthew 6:19-21 (KJV) says, "Lay not up for yourselves treasures upon earth, where moth and rust doth corrupt, and where thieves break through and steal: but lay up for yourselves treasures in heaven, where neither moth nor rust doth corrupt, and where thieves do not break through not steal: for where your treasure is, there will your heart be also." Where are you storing your treasures?

Jennings (Jay) Turner   2021

YOU BECOME LIKE WHAT YOU WORSHIP
NUGGET 124

Psalm 115: 3-8 (KJV) says, "But our God is in the heavens: He hath done whatsoever he hath pleased. Their idols are silver and gold, The work of men's hands. They have mouths, but they speak not: Eyes have they, but they see not: They have ears, but they hear not: Noses have they, but they smell not: They have hands, but they handle not: Feet have they, but they walk not: Neither speak they through their throat. They that make them are like unto them; So is every one that trusted in them."

Upon consideration, no one would wish to become more like false idols or gods that cannot give peace, wisdom nor eternal life. If we desire to become more like the one true God, we must worship him and make him our foremost priority. Who and what are you worshiping?

Jennings (Jay) Turner   2021

STAND FAST
NUGGET 125

Psalm 119:33-34 (MSG) says, "God, teach me lessons for living so I can stay the course. Give me insight so I can do what you tell me — my whole life one long, obedient response." Also, let us read 2 Thessalonians 2:13-16 (MSG) that says, "Meanwhile, we've got our hands full continually thanking God for you, our good friends — so loved by God! God picked you out as his from the very start. Think of it: included in God's original plan of salvation by the bond of faith in the living truth. This is the life of the Spirit he invited you to through the Message we delivered, in which you get in on the glory of our Master, Jesus Christ. So, friends, take a firm stand, feet on the ground and head high. Keep a tight grip on what you were taught, whether in personal conversation or by our letter."

In the Message we are encouraged to "stand firm." The King James version uses the words "stand fast." The scriptures tell us ways to help us to persevere while in the world. Therefore, study God's Word. Pray that the Holy Spirit will help you discern truth, and grow your faith that you may experience the joy and peace that comes with salvation. Also, the Church, that is, the saved who make up the body of Christ, should encourage and uphold one another. Use the Word as a response to those who would mock you.

Jesus is the cornerstone and foundation of Christianity. Stand fast upon his foundation. What foundation are relying on?

It has been said that a mighty oak tree is nothing more than an acorn that stood its ground.

Jennings (Jay) Turner   2021

HAS AMERICA GOTTEN SELF-RELIANT?
NUGGET 126

Please read the 16th chapter of the book of Ezekiel. God tells Ezekiel that he is to proclaim to Jerusalem her abominations. In the first 14 verses God tells how pitiful they were before he claimed them and greatly blessed them in every way. The more God blessed them with every tangible need, the less they felt the need to worship and rely on God. Then, beginning in verse 15, God begins to tell of their downfall. With wealth and plenty, they turned to their own ways. They began to trust in their own beauty and even used the silver, gold and jewels he had bestowed upon them to produce idols to worship. They replaced God with other desires and gods. After being patient, God judged them. He took away his blessings and allowed them to be overcome by all of their enemies.

I am 76 years old. In my lifetime, I detect a similar decline going on in our country. We have become extremely wealthy. The examples are almost endless. It is fine to enjoy our comforts and better living conditions but not if these things make us feel secure to the point of making us think that we can prosper and lead a full life without honoring God and being grateful for his provision. I believe that a large segment of our population trust in things other than God for all of its needs. In fact, there is an effort from many people, institutions, and even our government to push God away.

2 Chronicles 7:14 (KJV) says, "If my people, which are called by my name, shall humble themselves, and pray, and seek my face, and turn from their wicked ways; then will I hear from heaven, and will forgive their sin, and will heal their land." It is never too late to turn to God. Let's all pray, seek Gods face and expect a revival.

Jennings (Jay) Turner   2022

HELP THE POOR AND THE NEEDY
NUGGET 127

Luke 12:16-21 (MSG) says, "Then he told them this story: "The farm of a certain rich man produced a terrific crop. He talked to himself: 'What can I do? My barn isn't big enough for this harvest.' Then he said, 'Here's what I will do: I'll tear down my barns and build bigger ones. Then I'll gather in all my grain and goods, and I'll say to myself, Self, you've done well! You've got it made and can now retire. Take it easy and have the time of your life!' Just then God showed up and said, 'Fool! Tonight you die. And your barnful of goods-who gets it?' That's what happens when you fill your barn with Self and not with God."

Ezekiel 16:49-50 (MSG) says, "The sin of your sister Sodom was this: She lived with her daughters in the lap of luxury-proud, gluttonous, and lazy. They ignored the oppressed and the poor. They put on airs and lived obscene lives. And you know happened: I did away with them." The sin of Sodom was not only sexual deviation. They also ignored the oppressed and the poor.

I see quite a parallel between these two verses-and they are definitely speaking to me. Many of us are very affluent in material ways. As we grow in prosperity, we often build bigger homes (barns?), buy fancier cars, and on and on. Prosperity is not wrong, but it is important to remember the marginal, oppressed and the poor.

Finally, Matthew 6:19-21 (KJV) says,"Lay not up for yourselves treasures upon earth, where moth and rust doth corrupt, and where thieves break through and steal: but lay up for yourselves treasures in heaven, where neither moth nor rust doth corrupt, and where thieves do not break through nor steal: for where your treasure is, there will your heart be also."

Where are your treasures?

Jennings (Jay) Turner   2022

BUILD ON THE SURE FOUNDATION
NUGGET 128

Psalms 118:22 (NIV) says, "The stone the builders rejected has become the cornerstone." Acts 4:11 (NIV) reads, "Jesus is the stone you builders rejected, which has become the cornerstone." Jesus is the cornerstone, the foundation, upon which all lasting works must built upon. Let's move on to Luke and see what Jesus has to say about this. Luke 6:47-49 (NIV) says, "As for everyone who comes to me and hears my words and puts them into practice, I will show you what they are like. They are like a man building a house, who dug down deep and laid the foundation on rock. When a flood came, the torrent struck that house but could not shake it, because it was well built. But the one who hears my words and does not put them into practice is like a man who built a house on the ground without a foundation. The moment the torrent struck that house, it collapsed and its destruction was complete."

1 Corinthians 3:10-14 tells us that each of us should build with care upon the foundation of Jesus Christ. Everything we have built will be tried by fire. Each builder will receive a reward for whatever survives. The greatest achievement for anyone is to listen to the words of Jesus and put them into practice. What are you building upon the corner stone?

The reward is literally out of this world.

Jennings (Jay) Turner   2022

EXPECT OPPOSITION TO CHRISTIAN LIVING
NUGGET 129

When putting the words of Jesus into practice, we will undoubtedly face opposition. Enduring resistance, ridicule, or persecution is part of what it means to pick up and carry your cross. 1 John 3:1 (NIV) tells us,"See what great love the Father has lavished on us, that we should be called children of God! And that is what we are! The reason the world does not know us is that it did not know him." We find great encouragement in Matthew 5:10-12 (NIV) that reads, "Blessed are those who are persecuted because of righteousness, for theirs is the kingdom of heaven. Blessed are you when people insult you, persecute you and falsely say all kinds of evil against you because of me. Rejoice and be glad, because great is your reward in heaven, for in the same way they persecuted the prophets who were before you."

Maybe, if we never encounter any opposition, it is because we are listening and learning and not doing. Everyone has probably heard the advice to "dance like no one is watching." Another way to live is to "obey the teachings of Jesus because he is watching."

Jennings (Jay) Turner   2022

FREE TO WORSHIP
NUGGET 130

The story of God using Moses to charge Pharaoh that he let the Israelites go is found in the book of Exodus. God tells Moses exactly what to say to Pharaoh. Moses approaches Pharaoh with demands that are not met. The message of God, through Moses is to "set my people free." During the confrontations, Pharaoh is told that God's people are to be set free so that they may worship, sacrifice, feast, and serve their God. God performed wonders, including the deaths of every first-born child, to set his people free.

We in the United States are blessed to be able to seek God freely. This country was founded upon God with freedom being foundational. Indeed, religious freedom was a primary principle. God remarkably blessed our nation. A general falling away from the word of God has been evident during my lifetime. Did we become self assured? Did we think, "We can handle it from here?" I believe we are at a fork in the road. On one hand, we can get on our knees, repent, and seek God. Otherwise, we can go as we are and await the judgment that will surely come. We are free to worship, but how fervently do we take advantage of this God given opportunity? Should the blessings we enjoy cause us to become self absorbed, or should they spur us on to worship, serve, and seek our God?

Jennings (Jay) Turner   2022

JESUS' BODY AND BLOOD CAN COVER YOUR SIN
NUGGET 131

John chapter 2 is the account of Jesus turning water into wine. The amount of wine he provided was sufficient for all. Matthew 14:15-21 tells of how Jesus fed 5,000 men, besides women and children. After looking up to heaven, he blessed, and broke the five loaves and everyone did eat and were filled. There were even twelve baskets of fragments left over.

Mark 14:22-24 (KJV) says, "And as they did eat, Jesus took bread, and blessed, and brake it, and gave to them and said, Take, eat: this is my body. And he took the cup, and when he had given thanks, he gave it to them: and they all drank of it. And he said unto them, This is my blood of the new testament, which is shed for many." Jesus lived a sinless life thereby enabling him to be an acceptable sacrifice for our sins. Jesus willingly gave his life as a ransom for whosoever believes in him.

The bread represents his body which was broken for us. The wine represents his blood which was shed for us. As noted above, there is ample bread and wine for all. No matter how grievous our sins, the broken body and shed blood of Jesus are sufficient for anyone and everyone. This includes you and I. This is extraordinarily good news. Seek him today.

Jennings (Jay) Turner   2022

DON'T LET OTHERS CAUSE YOU TO STUMBLE
NUGGET 132

John the Baptist told Herod that it was unlawful for him to have his brother's wife Herodias. Therefore, Herod put John the Baptist in prison. After this, a birthday party for Herod was held. At the party, the daughter of Herodias danced before Herod and his guests and Herod was greatly pleased. He then promised the dancer that he would grant her whatsoever she asked. She requested that John the Baptist's head be brought to her in a charger. Her request saddened Herod. However, in order to save face in front of everyone gathered, he granted the request and the head of John the Baptist was brought to her.

The pull on Herod to save face with others influenced him to do that which he knew to be wrong. I wonder how many times I have compromised something in my faith journey because I went along with the crowd. My desire is to always speak up or step out for my Savior no matter what the circumstance or consequence. I pray that the Holy Spirit will help me to always to do so. My flesh is weak.

Jennings (Jay) Turner   2022.

NOT BY YOUR WORKS
NUGGET 133

Chapter 26 of Exodus speaks about the tabernacle. Verse 31 describes the veil that symbolizes Jesus. The veil is what separates the holy place from the most holy place. The high priest could only enter into the most holy place once a year with an offering for sins. This veil was blue, purple, and scarlet. It spoke to the deity, royalty and sacrifice of our lord Jesus Christ. In Matthew 27:51 we read that when Jesus died on the cross, this veil was rent in two from top to bottom. It was rent from the top, or above, because it was the work of God. It was rent so that you and I could now have access to the most holy place by passing through Jesus Christ.

This was and is all God's work. Ephesians 2:8-9 says, "For by grace are ye saved through faith; and that not of yourselves: it is the gift of God: not of works, lest any man should boast." John 6:28-29 says, "Then they said unto him, what shall we do, that we might work the works of God? Jesus answered and said unto them, 'This is the work of God, that ye believe on him whom he hath sent'"

Because of God's great love and grace, he gave us his only son Jesus to be the sacrifice for our sins if we will only believe in him. What are you working at or believing in to save you from your sins?

Jennings (Jay) Turner   2022

THE CHURCH IS THE BODY OF CHRIST
NUGGET 134

In Acts chapter 9 Jesus asks Saul (soon to be Paul) why he is persecuting him. Saul had not yet met Jesus. Therefore, how could he be persecuting him? It was because the Church is the body of Jesus and Saul had been persecuting the Church. The true Church is the body of believers of the risen Lord Jesus Christ. The true Church is not a building or denomination. It is the body of believers who have their names written in the Lamb's Book of Life.

Do you believe that you are a sinner? Do you believe that Jesus died on the cross in order to pay the price for your sins? Do you believe that Jesus has risen from the dead and is sitting at the right hand of God? Have you desired to leave your sin? If you answered "yes" to these questions, call upon Jesus and your name will be entered into the Lamb's book of life. Thus begins your eternal life with him. A life wherein you are a part of the body of Jesus.

Jennings (Jay) Turner   2022

DON'T FOLLOW FROM AFAR
NUGGET 135

Chapter 22 of Luke's gospel tells of the betrayal of Jesus by Judas. Verse 54 (KJV) says, "Then took they him, and led him, and brought him into the high priest's house. And Peter followed afar off." Before morning, Peter would deny Jesus three times. A lesson here is not to put any distance between yourself and Jesus whether to do so may appear to be convenient.

Yesterday's mess can become today's message. Your test can become your testimony.

Jennings (Jay) Turner   2022

HAPPINESS OR JOY
NUGGET 136

To most people, happiness seems to be based on happenings. That is, what is going on around them. In Philippians 1:21 Paul writes, "For to me to live is Christ, and to die is gain." It is apparent in Paul's letters that he possesses joy in spite of the many hardships he faced during his earthly ministry. Paul had been beaten, stoned, put into chains, imprisoned, shipwrecked, and scourged.

Paul's joy was based on what was going on inside him and not what was going on around him. Everything changed for Paul when he encountered Jesus. Each of us has the opportunity to encounter Jesus. He stands at the door and knocks. If you will but open the door, he will come in unto you. Christians are in the world but not of the world (John 17:19). Never let anything that is of this world, whether tangible or intangible, get between you and God. There is joy and peace that passes all understanding available to anyone who will call upon the Lord.

Jennings (Jay) Turner   2023

CHEERFULLY SHARE
NUGGET 137

In Matthew 16:9-10 (KJV) Jesus reminds the disciples about how five loaves of bread fed five thousand people and how seven loaves had fed four thousand. He also reminds them of how the amount of bread left over exceeded what they had started with. A lesson here may be that when we give of what we have, it will be enough for both the recipients and ourselves. Whenever possible, we should all be generous and kind. How can you share some of the gifts you've been given with others?

Being kind is love in work clothes (Nicky Gumbel)

Jennings (Jay) Turner   2023

SPIRITUAL JOURNEY
NUGGET 138

Egypt is the symbol of the world in the Old Testament. It was the center of all things temporal. God took his people out of Egypt in what we know as the Exodus. They were headed to Canaan which was the promised land. In terms of distance it was not far. Ideally, this might have been a short trip but his people were not ready for it. For forty years they faced trials and testings as God was preparing them for the promised land. God was always with his people during their journey and the same is true of Christians today. We can trust him to always be with us during our troubles. Stand firm and know that he wishes us to become more like Jesus. How is your journey going?

Jennings (Jay) Turner   2023

OUT OF LOVE COMES JOY
NUGGET 139

Shortly before his betrayal, a woman poured out expensive perfume on Jesus. The perfume was worth about a year's wages. Some present at the time believed this was a foolish act. Their reasoning was that the perfume could have been sold and the proceeds given to the poor. Jesus, however, commended her and said that she would be remembered for her act of kindness. Jesus finds joy in whatever we do out of love for him. What act of kindness can you think of to do out of love for Jesus that will bring him joy?

Jennings (Jay) Turner   2023

GOOD FRUIT
NUGGET 140

In Luke, chapter 3, John The Baptist tells the multitude coming to be baptized to "bring forth therefore fruits worthy of repentance." In verse 9 John says, "And now also the axe is laid unto the root of the trees: every tree therefore which brings not forth good fruit is hewn down, and cast into the fire." In verse 10 the people asked him, saying, "What shall we do then?" John's response is in verse 11, "He answereth and saith unto them, He that hath two coats, let him impart to him that hath none; and he that hath meat, let him do likewise."

Salvation cannot be gained or earned through good works. John tells us that good fruit is a natural result of repentance. Helping the poor, the needy and the hungry are examples of good fruit that can result from repentance. What examples of good fruit are apparent in your life?

Jennings (Jay) Turner   2023

BE HAPPY WITH GOD'S PROVISION
NUGGET 141

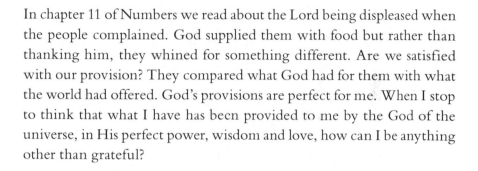

In chapter 11 of Numbers we read about the Lord being displeased when the people complained. God supplied them with food but rather than thanking him, they whined for something different. Are we satisfied with our provision? They compared what God had for them with what the world had offered. God's provisions are perfect for me. When I stop to think that what I have has been provided to me by the God of the universe, in His perfect power, wisdom and love, how can I be anything other than grateful?

Jennings (Jay) Turner   2023

SERVANT ATTITUDE
NUGGET 142

The bible is filled with examples of praying to God for help in all kinds of situations. The Psalms are filled with examples. Especially David's many cries to God to provide assistance. God should always be our first source when seeking guidance, answers or help. However, rather than praying that God will do something for you, do you sometimes pray that God will do something for others through you? Let us all pray that God will use us as a tool to help others.

Jennings (Jay) Turner   2023

ETERNAL GOOD WORKS
NUGGET 143

In Matthew 21:42 (KJV) Jesus says, "Did ye never read in the scriptures, The stone which the builders rejected, The same is become the head of the corner?" Also, 1 Corinthians 3:11-14 (KJV) reads, "For other foundation can no man lay than that is laid, which is Jesus Christ. Now if any man build upon this foundation gold, silver, precious stones, wood, hay, stubble; every man's work shall be made manifest: for the day shall declare it, because it shall be revealed by fire; and fire shall try every man's work of what sort it is. If any man's work abide which he hath built thereupon, he shall receive a reward."

I suggest that we should all put our primary emphasis on building upon the foundation of Jesus Christ things and works that will be eternal. These eternal building blocks might include: sharing the gospel, feeding the hungry, helping the poor and marginalized, and loving others as ourselves. In general, we should keep searching the scriptures, pray for guidance, and obey the leading of the Holy Spirit.

Do not place your emphasis on things that are temporal. What building blocks that are eternal are you adding to the foundation which is Jesus Christ?

Jennings (Jay) Turner   2023

A RIGHT RELATIONSHIP
NUGGET 144

Romans 4:13 (NLT) says, "Clearly, God's promise to give the whole earth to Abraham and his descendants was based not on his obedience to God's law, but on a right relationship with God that comes by faith." This verse indicates that in order to have a relationship with God, you must have faith. Abraham's faith was made manifest by his actions (works). He even obeyed to the point of offering Isaac upon an altar. Is our faith resulting in actions? James 2:20 indicates that faith without works is dead. Just wishing the poor and the hungry well without helping is a faith that is dead. Some people may assign a committee to study the problem. I pray that each of us will ask the Holy Spirit to help us to see and to seize opportunities in order to put feet upon our faith.

Jennings (Jay) Turner   2023

SCRIPTURE SHOULD BE A MIRROR
NUGGET 145

It is humbling to look into the scriptures as if looking into a mirror and ask the Holy Spirit to reveal what we may have to work upon. We can all use a tune-up. I am ready to have some oil added and maybe get realigned.

Jennings (Jay) Turner   2023

ABRAHAM TESTED
NUGGET 146

In the twenty second chapter of Genesis we are told of how God tested Abraham when he told him that he was to offer his son Isaac for a burnt offering. Genesis 22:3-5 (NLT) reads, "The next morning Abraham got up early. He saddled this donkey and took two of his servants with him along with his son Isaac. Then he chopped wood for a fire for a burnt offering and set out for the place God had told him about. On the third day of their journey, Abraham looked up and saw the place in the distance. 'Stay here with the donkey' Abraham told the servants. 'The boy and I will travel a little farther. We will worship there, and then we will come right back.'"

In this story, Abraham is carrying a knife and fire and Isaac is carrying wood. Abraham is willing, if necessary, to sacrifice his son but his faith that God would provide himself a sacrifice is not lacking and we can see it when he tells the servants "we" will be back.

God did provide himself a sacrifice. Abraham looked up and saw a ram caught by its horns in a thicket. This must have been a foreshadow of when God would provide himself, in the form of his Son. Jesus also had his head surrounded by thorns.

What amazing love! It is only reasonable to accept this love and pass it on in every way imaginable. How can you pass it on?

Jennings (Jay) Turner   2023

VALLEYS ARE LUSH WITH GROWTH
NUGGET 147

People often use the term "mountain top experience" to describe an experience or happening that has been especially satisfying. The word "valley" is often associated with a situation that isn't pleasant. However, if you actually visit and observe mountain tops and valleys, you will find that the mountain top has only sparse growth while the valley is much more lush. I believe that this is a metaphor for our spiritual lives. I have grown closer to my Lord during valley experiences than when everything is smooth. We can all do well to regard unpleasant circumstances as chances to grow in anticipation of the ultimate mountain top experience of eternity with our Savior.

Mountain tops inspire us but valleys mature us (Nicky Gumbel)

Jennings (Jay) Turner   2023

GIVING ATTITUDE
NUGGET 148

Worldly people are always wanting what they don't have. Mature Christians are always giving what they do have.

The gospel is good news. Jesus is knocking at the door of your heart. Open the door and he will come in. Come and see how good this news is.

Jennings (Jay) Turner   2023

NOTHING CAN SEPARATE YOU
NUGGET 149

When the disciples denied Jesus and ran from his crucifixion, he still came to them. Nothing can separate you from Jesus. Salvation is available to you because of God's plan. His great grace, mercy and love resulted in his only son, our Lord Jesus Christ, becoming the only satisfactory sacrifice that could pay for our sins. All we need to do is believe and ask him to save us. No amount of works could ever earn our salvation. We must come to the Father through Jesus.

Jennings (Jay) Turner   2023

GUARD YOUR EYES
NUGGET 150

Please read Luke 11:34-36. Your eyes are the light and lamp into your heart and soul. Be careful what you are looking at. We are surrounded by countless ungodly influences. Take time to look into God's Word daily. Try to gather with other believers for worship and fellowship weekly. These activities not only help to keep us focused, but they bring blessings. Iron sharpens iron. Come and see.

Jennings (Jay) Turner   2023

JESUS IS THE ROCK
NUGGET 151

You may shake with anxiety and fear but the Rock doesn't. Hide yourself in the cleft of the Rock. Jesus was "cleft" for us when he suffered on the cross. He is the "Rock of Ages." Trust in him. He is worthy. What are YOU trusting in?

Jennings (Jay) Turner   2023

TEMPLE OF GOD
NUGGET 152

1 Corinthians 6:19 (NLT) says, "Don't you realize that your body is the temple of the Holy Spirit, who lives in you and was given to you by God? You do not belong to yourself." If we are his temple (house) then we live for others. Therefore, never close your doors.

Jennings (Jay) Turner   2023

WHEEL METAPHOR
NUGGET 153

Let's imagine that our life is a ride in a car. I would like us to think of two different wheels. One is the spare tire that is kept in the trunk. It is probably not even in sight. We really never think about it. We don't even check on it before starting our journey. It is only there for our use when and if we experience a pretty bad problem. Even then, many of us would call someone to come and mount this spare wheel. Once the problem has passed, it can simply be put back into its place.

The second wheel for us to consider is the steering wheel. This wheel is used to keep our car heading in the correct direction so that we will arrive at a destination.

If God is in our life, and along for the ride through our life, how do we see Him in this metaphor? Do we wish to engage Him in our ride only when we are stuck or do we ask for His leading in our life and allow Him to be the steering wheel? I'll bet all of us, during our journey, have gone down a wrong road we wish we could have avoided. Are you ready to allow God to steer you? Enjoy the ride and see where it takes you. No backseat driving and quit asking if we are there yet!

Jennings (Jay) Turner   2023

CRUISE SHIP OR A RESCUE VESSEL?
NUGGET 154

The analogy is very simple: a local church should not spend an inordinate amount or resources making the "ship" more alluring and comfortable for its passengers at the expense of its first mission: that of saving lost souls that are adrift and drowning in the surrounding sea of sin. I am not suggesting that a nice building with amenities is necessarily wrong any more than having wealth is wrong. The important thing is to always remain sensitive to the Holy Spirit and not allow anything to blur the number one mission. The first priority should not be to make the voyage as comfortable as humanly possible. We must always be cautious that Jesus is at the helm and that the rudder is the Holy Spirit. Sometimes, even when one of the ships has hit an iceberg, the crew and passengers appear to be most concerned with straightening up the deck chairs.

I envision a rescue vessel as being streamlined, maneuverable, and constantly in search of potentially lost souls in need of saving. I also imagine the entire crew has been carefully trained in life saving techniques. Each crew member has a lifeline with a flotation device attached. They know just where to throw it. Upon the life ring is the words "Jesus Saves". All of the crew members realize that they themselves were once adrift and lost, and by grace, they heard the call and accepted the free gift that was offered. They clearly shout out the gospel message. They love their job and have given themselves wholly to it. They are joyous that they have gifted their lives to do the will of the One who owns the ship and guides it along. They make no judgments whatsoever about to whom they will throw a lifeline. They love everyone in trouble in the sea. They pay no attention to the outer appearance of the people in the sea because without this ship they will be forever lost. The name of the rescue vessel is "Salvation". All anyone in the sea must do to be saved is, by faith, take hold of the life ring (named Jesus) that is freely offered to all. Many in the sea are hanging on to alternative floating devices. These floating devices have many different names upon them. Some of the names include; money, position, pride, fame, family, addiction, etc. It is very sad that so many will perish rather than let go of something that cannot, in the end, save them. By letting go, they would be free to accept eternal life and begin the finest voyage anyone can take. The final port of resting for these passengers is *out of this world*. Oh yes!

Jennings (Jay) Turner. 2019

DOING IT YOUR WAY?
NUGGET 155

In Jeremiah chapter 42 is the story of a remnant of Judah who approached the prophet. The remnant asked Jeremiah to pray to God concerning whether they should go into Egypt to escape their enemies. This remnant, led by Johanan, assured Jeremiah that they would do whatever God directed. God's answer was that if they went into Egypt they would be slain with the sword, pestilence, and famine. However, if they would remain in Judah, he would bless them and protect them. Regardless of God's promises, they went down into Egypt. It appears obvious that they had their mind made up all along but wanted support for the decision they had already made.

Do we seek God's will so that we can see if it agrees with our plan? It took me a long time to realize that whatever God's plan for me may be, his plan is the very best one for me to follow. His love for me is so overwhelming that he sent his son to die for my sins. His plan will always be in my best interest and, better yet, will bring him glory. The key is to seek his plan before you make your plan.

Jennings (Jay) Turner 2021

Printed in the United States
by Baker & Taylor Publisher Services